UNDERSTANDING SCRIPTURE

Studies in Judaism and Christianity

Exploration of Issues in the Contemporary Dialogue Between Christians and Jews

Editor in Chief for
Stimulus Books
Helga Croner

Editors
Lawrence Boadt, C.S.P.
Helga Croner
Leon Klenicki
John Koenig
Kevin A. Lynch, C.S.P.

 A STIMULUS BOOK

UNDERSTANDING SCRIPTURE

Explorations of Jewish and Christian Traditions of Interpretation

Clemens Thoma and Michael Wyschogrod, editors

A STIMULUS BOOK

PAULIST PRESS ♦ NEW YORK ♦ MAHWAH

Library of Congress Cataloging-in-Publication Data

Understanding scripture.

    (A Stimulus book)
    Includes index.
    1. Bible—Hermeneutics. 2. Christianity and other religions—Judaism. 3. Judaism—Relations—Christianity. I. Thoma, Clemens, 1932-
II. Wyschogrod, Michael, 1928-
BS476.U48   1986   220.6'01   86-30630
ISBN 0-8091-2873-X (pbk.)

Published by Paulist Press
997 Macarthur Boulevard
Mahwah, N.J. 07430

Printed and bound in the United States of America

Contents

I. TRADITION AND INSPIRATION IN SCRIPTURE

II. EXEGETICAL TRADITIONS

Abbreviations

AAS	Acta Apostolicae Sedis
AnBib	Analecta biblica (Rome)
CSEL	Corpus scriptorum ecclesiasticorum latinorum (Vienna)
M	Mishna
TB	Babylonian Talmud
TJ	Talmud of Jerusalem (Palestinian)
U.T.	Ugaritic Textbook (Rome, 1965)

Hebrew Terms

derash   homiletic meaning

halakha   (halakh = to go) a way to go, a way of living, the
                      prescriptive portions of the Torah

middot   rabbinic principles of biblical interpretation

parshanut ha-Miqra exposition of Scripture

peshat   literal meaning, simple meaning

piyyut   liturgical poetry

Torah she-be'alpeh oral Torah

Torah she-biktav   written Torah

INTRODUCTION

Introduction

Clemens Thoma
Michael Wyschogrod

The interaction between Judaism and Christianity finds itself today in a delicate stage of its development. It is clear that much has been accomplished. Meetings between Jewish and Christian religious bodies are no longer a rarity, and this alone—even in the absence of changes in religious teachings—would not be without significance since sustained human contact tends to undermine negative stereotypes.

The fact is, of course, that contacts have led to the reconsideration of a number of doctrines widely accepted in earlier times in Christendom but today rejected by a growing body of Christian opinion. Among such doctrines are the views that the Jews are collectively responsible for the death of Jesus and that the Church, as the New Israel, has superseded the election of the old Israel. While, for a variety of reasons, such specific changes are harder to point to on the Jewish side, there too we can observe a weakening of the conviction that Christians are necessarily antisemites whose real aim is to persuade all Jews to accept baptism.

In short, it is undeniable that there has been progress since the end of World War II, which marked the beginning of a new era in Jewish-Christian relations. And yet, one also senses that the relationship has entered a rather delicate phase. There are various reasons for this. To some extent, this is the result of the successes that have been achieved. Once the level of expectation is raised, expectations can easily surpass results. Religious communities bound by loyalty to revealed Scriptures find rapid change particularly difficult. Were it otherwise, revelation would not be taken seriously. And finally, there is the political dimension that has played an important role in the Jewish-Christian dialogue in recent decades.

3

The presence of a political dimension in the relation between Judaism and Christianity, and particularly in the relation between Judaism and the Roman Catholic Church, should surprise no one. It is widely agreed that the current phase of Jewish-Christian relations dawned after the facts of the Holocaust were absorbed into the consciousness of Jews and Christians. It is therefore a political event—the greatest mass-murder in history—in whose shadow the dialogue has proceeded for the last four decades.

With the creation of the State of Israel which absorbed many Holocaust survivors, an additional political dimension was added to the relation between Jews and Roman Catholics because the Holy See, the center of the Roman Catholic Church, has not yet established normal diplomatic relations with Israel. In light of these factors, it would be unrealistic to ignore the political dimension of Jewish-Catholic relations.

As can be expected, the political dimension has not been ignored. Instrumentalities for interaction between Jewish organizations and the Vatican have been created. There are periodic meetings at which a wide variety of issues of common concern are treated. And while there generally is some scholarly presence at these meetings, the scholarly agenda is not central. This should not be a cause for surprise.

The Jewish agencies that participate in these official meetings are Jewish defense agencies. Their task is to fight antisemitism and to protect human rights, including Jewish rights, wherever threatened. Theological scholarship as such is not a central interest for them, except to the extent that Christian theology serves to feed antisemitism.

In the fall of 1982, the editors of this volume discovered that they were of one mind in their view that the current state of the Jewish-Catholic conversation was incomplete. We recognized that the political dimension of the relation between Jews and Catholics needed to be dealt with, and we were glad that it was dealt with on an official level. But we were not happy to observe that the limited amount of scholarly interaction that was taking place occurred in a political context. We were even more unhappy to observe that there was no forum in which Jews and Catholics met as scholars to discuss scholarly issues without overt or covert political agendas. We were convinced that, important as social and political issues are, the center of Jewish-Catholic relations had to be located in an exchange of views about issues of common scholarly concern, conducted in an atmosphere of respect for the views of all concerned and dedication to the standards of historical and theological research. Genuine scholarship cannot thrive in an emotional atmosphere, whether of mutual suspicion or uncritical affection.

In order to explore the possibilities of remedying the situation, we initiated a correspondence with Msgr. (now Bishop) Jorge Mejia, then Secretary of the Vatican Commission for Religious Relations with the Jews. Toward the end of 1982, after consulting with Mr. Henry Siegman, Executive Director of the American Jewish Congress, we traveled to Rome where we met with Msgr. Mejia and Bishop Ramon Torrella, Vice-President of the Commission for Promoting Christian Unity.

We agreed to create an academic forum for Jewish-Christian scholarly research that would focus on topics central to the two faiths. It would be sponsored by the Institute for Jewish-Christian Relations of the American Jewish Congress, and the Institute for Jewish-Christian Research of the Theological Faculty of Lucerne, the latter acting in consultation and collaboration with the Vatican Commission for Religious Relations with the Jews. This formula, we felt, would express the scholarly character of the future consultations while signifying the Vatican's commitment to the enterprise. Our aim was to achieve an interchange of ideas by those who were academically competent and free to pursue the truth uninfluenced by extraneous considerations. This volume is the first result of our joint enterprise.

Its genesis was a consultation held from January 16 to 18, 1984 in Lucerne, Switzerland, devoted to "The Authority and Interpretation of Scripture in Judaism and Christianity." The choice of topic hardly needs justification. Judaism and Christianity are the only two faiths that share a Scripture which they both read as the word of God. While it is clear that their interpretations of these common Scriptures have diverged, it must also be noted that the sharing of a common authoritative text—even if differently interpreted—is an extraordinarily significant fact for each religion. Fully cognizant of a difficult history behind us, we decided to begin a search for the truth as befits scholars and members of our respective religious communities.

Some of the papers in this volume were circulated and delivered in preliminary form at the Lucerne meeting and revised in light of the discussion, while others were written after the meeting, inspired both by the papers delivered and by the ensuing discussion. Among them, they examine a wide range of issues of biblical interpretation in the two communities.

At a reception for the participants of the Consultation, Bishop Dr. Otto Wuest of Basel addressed the following words to Msgr. (now Bishop) Jorge Mejia, the representative of the Vatican:

The Church of Basel and the Church of Switzerland as a whole, my dear Msgr., does not understand itself as a provincial Church, but as part of the Church that wishes and is able to contribute to the whole Church. I am pleased that we were able to take the initiative, in juxtaposition to the central authorities of the Church, with respect to these important questions that concern the Church and Judaism, for the benefit of both Jews and Christians. We need scholarship if we wish to establish the relationship between Judaism and Christianity permanently on a solid foundation.

It is toward building that permanent foundation of scholarly research in the spirit of religious understanding that this volume is dedicated.

I. TRADITION AND INSPIRATION IN SCRIPTURE

The Authority and Interpretation of Scripture in Jewish Tradition

Nahum M. Sarna

1. THE ROLE OF SCRIPTURE IN JEWISH CIVILIZATION

"The Holy Scriptures may not be read but may be studied, and lectures on them given. . . ."[1]

Although this tannaitic statement is a halakhic ruling within the context of the Sabbath laws, yet, if disengaged from its immediate reference, and taken as an abstract formulation, it expresses a profound truth. For the Bible cannot be read; it can only be studied and expounded.

This none-too-obvious, yet incontrovertible, fact is to be accounted for partly as a product of a particular historical circumstance. The flood-tides of Hellenism engulfed the ancient Near Eastern world and transformed its civilization, so that the cultural environment that produced the Hebrew Bible was no longer familiar to the reader. Thereafter, the traditional metaphors of biblical thought ceased to be immediately intelligible, and the biblical text ceased to be instantly readable; it could only be studied and expounded.

But there is much more to it than this. The very fact that the Hebrew Scriptures, the canonized, definitively fixed body of sacred literature, became the focus, long the exclusive focus, of Jewish cultural activity, and constituted the very protoplasm of Jewish existence, the matrix out of which emerged all subsequent development—this fact inevitably predetermined the approach to the text. The interpretation thereof was informed by the ever-abiding consciousness that it was the major source for the national language, the well-spring of the peculiar life-style of the Jew, the font of Jewish values, ideals and hopes. These were matters of transcendent seriousness that demanded not surface reading but deep study and interpretation, and interpretation itself became a

9

propaedeutic discipline indispensable to the training of the cultivated Jew. As Gershom Scholem pointed out, commentary on Scripture became "the characteristic expression of Jewish thinking about truth."[2] The unbelievably rich hermeneutical literature subsumed generically under the rubric of *parshanut ha-Miqra,* the exposition of the Scriptures, supplies all the essential ingredients of Jewish intellectual and spiritual history. A product of over two millennia of intensive intellectual activity, it is characterized by infinitely variegated attitudes and approaches—with a refusal to absolutize any single stance.[3]

Rabbinic exegesis is firmly grounded in the cardinal principle that embedded in the sacred text is a multiplicity of meanings, the full richness of which cannot be expressed through a single body of doctrine or by any monolithic system that is logically self-consistent. To the contrary, the intrinsic, endless variety of interpretation, even if, or perhaps especially because, it may be internally contradictory and replete with antinomies, reinforced the reality of the divine inspiration behind the text. The sages of the Talmud vividly expressed the matter this way: The prophet Jeremiah proclaimed: " 'Behold, My word is like fire—declares the Lord—and like a hammer that shatters rock' (Jer. 23:29). Just as a hammer shatters rock into numerous splinters, so may a single biblical verse yield a multiplicity of meanings."[4] This same concept is expressed in several ways, whether as: "There are seventy facets to the Torah,"[5] the number, of course, being typological and communicating comprehensiveness, or whether as, in the words of the tanna Ben Bag-Bag, "Turn it over, turn it over, for everything is in it."[6]

All this means, of course, that for more than two thousand years the Hebrew Bible has been accepted and studied by Jews as the seminal body of religious literature, which has been filtered through a continuous process of rabbinic interpretation and reinterpretation within the community of practice and faith whence its immediate authority derived.

2. RABBINIC EXEGESIS

Already in the year 553 C.E., the emperor Justinian took note of this fact in his *novella constitutio* concerning the Jews to whom he granted permission to read their sacred Scriptures in Greek, Latin or any other language. He stipulated, however, that they should "read the holy words themselves, rejecting the commentaries" by which he clearly meant rabbinic exegesis. As Justinian put it, "the so-called second tradition *(deuterosis)* we prohibit entirely, for it is not part of the sacred books nor is it handed down by divine inspiration through the prophets, but the handiwork of men, speaking only of earthly things and having nothing of the divine in it.''[7]

Justinian's motives and purposes are irrelevant to the present theme, for they belong within the category of medieval Jewish-Christian polemics. But this specified restriction does illustrate an historic fact of cardinal importance that differentiates the Jewish study of the Scriptures from the Christian approach which, of course, has its own venerable tradition of theological reinterpretation of the Bible of the Jews. The literate, committed Jew, to whom the study of the Bible is at one and the same time a religious obligation, a spiritual exercise, a mode of worship, and a moral as well as an intellectual discipline, is confronted with a vast array of texts which are not in themselves authoritative, yet which command attention, concentrated thought, and study. Jewish scriptural exegesis is a literature that has become endowed with a life and energy of its own, and in its independent existence the light of the Hebrew Bible has become refracted through a thousand prisms. To my mind, the most noble expression of rabbinic Judaism is the Great Rabbinic Bible exemplified by Jacob b. Hayyim's edition of 1524/25.[8] What I mean is that the Hebrew text is surrounded by a sea of commentaries of diverse authorship, provenance, dating and exegetical approaches, often mutually incompatible, all of which coexist peacefully within the confines of a single page, all accommodated within the framework of a single tradition. To use rabbinic parlance, ''The one and the other alike are the words of the living God.''[9]

3. INNER BIBLICAL EXEGESIS

At this point, I wish to advance the thesis that the traditional Jewish approach to the text as a living organism that perpetually rejuvenates and transforms itself was not a rabbinic innovation but a continuation of an established process that was contemporaneous with the formation of biblical literature itself. Recent studies in the concept of "Canon" have focused attention upon a hitherto neglected aspect of the subject. There is "Canon" as the formal expression of religio-legal decision-making on the part of some ecclesiastical body—about which, incidentally, we know next to nothing. But there is also "canon" as a dynamic process whereby a text, once it is recognized as being Scripture, necessarily and spontaneously generates interpretation and adaptation so that often the original text is transformed into a new and expanded text.[10] Thus is created inner-biblical exegesis.[11] As a matter of fact, it may be noted that even the Canon in the traditional, formal, sense of the word as a delimited, definitive and authoritative body of literature is ultimately a product of exegetical activity as is even more so the internal, final arrangement of the books in both Jewish and Christian traditions. The conclusion of the Hebrew Scriptures with Chronicles makes a statement that the consummation of history involves the ideal of the return of the Jewish people to its land, of the restoration of Jewish sovereignty and of spiritual renewal.[12] The arrangement of what Christians call the "Old Testament" so that it closes with the words of the prophet Malachi interprets the coming of Elijah and the "great and awesome day of the Lord" in 3:23 as proleptic of the New Testament in which the role of John the Baptist and the advent of the Christian Messiah is pivotal.

It seems to me that an excellent example of the process of inner-biblical exegesis being discernible within the Scriptures themselves, and being continued in rabbinic and medieval exegesis, is to be found in Gen. 21:33 which informs us that Abraham "planted a tamarisk *('eshel)* at Beer-sheba and invoked there the name of the LORD, the everlasting God." Now this passage is extraordinary in that the action of the patriarch appears to be in contradiction to the strict prohibition in the Torah on the cultic use of trees[13] and on the planting of a tree near the altar of God.[14] The phenomenon of the sacred tree, particularly one associated with a hallowed site, is well known in a variety of cultures. Sometimes the tree is a medium of oracles and divination, to which names like *'elon moreh,* "the terebinth of the oracle-giver" in Gen. 12:6, and *'elon me'onenim,* "the terebinth of the soothsayers" in Judg. 9:37, are witness. Sometimes fertility cults flourished in connection with these trees, a form of paganism that seems to have been very attractive to many Israelites.[15] In light of all this, it is remarkable that the tradition about Abraham planting a tamarisk and invoking there the name of the Lord should appear in the Abrahamic biography, and not have been expunged.

A close look at the text reveals that the narrative already exhibits a sensitivity to the problem. Firstly, the descriptive title of God is given as *'el 'olam.* This epithet appears nowhere else in the Bible, but *'olam* is known to be one of the Canaanite divine titles.[16] Yet the God whom Abraham worshiped is explicitly named YHWH, using the tetragrammaton, the exclusive name for the God of Israel. Secondly, unlike the other instances of the use of the formula, "He invoked the name of the LORD,"[17] the usual concomitant of altar building is, tellingly, here omitted. A subtle process of inner-biblical exegesis is at work in order to disengage Abraham's act from the Canaanite cults.

4. RABBINIC TRANSFORMATIONS

How has this passage fared at the hands of rabbinic commentators? At first glance, the exegesis appears to be so naive as to be worthy of immediate dismissal. In T.B. Sotah 10a[18] we read that R. Nehemiah interpreted *'eshel,* not as a tamarisk but as a hospice.[19] Abraham, he said, received wayfarers there, providing them with food and shelter, and bringing them closer to God. To add force to this interpretation, *'eshel* is even taken as an acronym from *'akhilah, šetiyah, linah,* "eating, drinking and lodging the night."[20] All this, of course, is fanciful eisegesis but what is seminal is that rabbinic and medieval commentary have extended the process of inner-biblical exegesis, thereby reinterpreting Abraham's cultic act to endow it with profound pedagogic value. An incident belonging to the realm of man's individual personal approach to God in a ritual ambience has been so transformed that it now exemplifies God's demands on man in a socio-moral context. The provision of wayfarers is itself elevated to being a mode of divine worship.

At times, rabbinic and medieval Jewish exegesis give every appearance of constituting critiques of biblical morality. The story of Noah is a case in point. The text of Gen. 6:9 declares him to be a perfectly righteous man. Nevertheless, the silence of Noah, and his seeming unconcern for the fate of his fellow human beings, contrast strikingly with Abraham's vocal and passionate plea for the lives of his contemporaries in Sodom and Gomorrah. Rabbinic sensitivity to what appears to be a moral flaw in his character expresses itself in two ways. On the one hand, *Genesis Rabba* 30:7 has Noah building the ark for no less than one hundred and twenty years,[21] all the while preaching to his compatriots and calling on them to repent of their evil ways;[22] on the other hand, some sages did not hesitate to characterize Noah as being among those of little faith, and to relativize his righteous state. They were careful to note that the text itself appears to qualify its verdict on Noah's moral condition by the careful formulation "He was righteous *in his generation*"; had he lived in the days of Abraham, he would not have been significant.[23]

Another example of this type of critical approach may be found in the treatment of the story of the kidnaping of Sarai, as told in Gen. 12:11–20. Abram is fearful of the evil of which human beings are capable. In order to save his own life, he appears to place the honor of his wife in jeopardy through misrepresentation of their relationship. Sarai's collusion may be looked upon as an act of self-sacrifice on behalf of her husband, but how is Abram's conduct to be judged? It is instructive to compare the reactions of some modern commentators with that of their medieval counterparts.

S. R. Driver remarks: "Untruthfulness and dissimulation are extremely common faults in the east; and it would be manifestly unjust to measure Abram by Christian standards."[24]

H. E. Ryle tells us: "It is repellent to our sense of honor, chivalry and purity. . . . This story doubtless would not have appeared so sordid to the ancient Israelites as it does to us. Perhaps the cunning, the deception and the increase of wealth may have commended the story to the Israelites of old times . . . the moral of the story does not satisfy any Christian standard in its representation of either Jehovah or of the patriarch."[25]

J. Skinner notes: "There is no suggestion that either the untruthfulness or the selfish cowardice of the request was severely reprobated by the ethical code to which the narrative appealed. . . ."[26]

Now let us turn to the treatment of the problem as presented in the comentaries of Nahmanides (RaMBaN, 1194–1270) and David Kimhi (?1160–1235?). The former unequivocally declares:

"Know that our father Abraham inadvertently committed a great offense in that he placed his virtuous wife in jeopardy of sin because of his fear of being killed. He should have trusted in God to save him, his wife and all he had, for God has the power to help and to save. . . . On account of this act, his descendants were doomed to suffer the Egyptian exile at the hand of Pharaoh" (ad loc.).

David Kimhi first observes that had Abraham been aware of the ugliness of the Egyptians and of their being steeped in immorality he would never have gone to Egypt in the first place, but would rather have suffered famine than jeopardize his wife. In the circumstances, however, in which the patriarch now finds himself, says Kimhi, in effect, he is confronted with a moral dilemma and forced to make a choice between two evils: should he disclose the truth, he would assuredly be killed, and Sarai, beautiful and unprotected in an alien society of low moral standards, would certainly be condemned to life-long shame and degradation. If, however, he resorts to subterfuge, she might be violated by some Egyptian, but at least husband and wife would both survive. It would not have been proper, adds Kimhi, to have relied on a miracle as an excuse for inaction.

Whatever be the shortcomings of Kimhi's interpretation, it is clear that, unlike modern commentators, he sees the patriarch faced with a very real moral problem. Abraham's decision involved a conflict between human life and human dignity and their respective positions within a hierarchy of values. Unlike the above-cited moderns, he does not confuse chivalry with morality. What is of significance is that both Nahmanides and Kimhi are sensitive to a problem of biblical morality.

One final example is the thoroughly repellent folk-narrative, preserved in 2 Kings 2:23–24, about the prophet Elisha. Following his miraculous curing of the polluted waters of Jericho, the prophet made his way to Bethel. Some little children poked fun at his baldheadedness. Elisha pronounced a curse upon them in the name of the Lord, whereupon two bears came out of the woods and mangled forty-two children.

What did the rabbis do with this story? By the time they were through with it, nothing means what it appears to mean on the surface.[27] The "children" are not minors but of the age of moral responsibility. Note that the text initially describes the offenders as *ne'arim*, which in biblical Hebrew is an indeterminate noun that can cover a three month baby, as in Exod. 2:6, and a grown man, as in 2 Chron. 13:7. Moreover, a play on the verbal form of the word suggests that these people were *meno'arim min ha-mitsvot*, "they had divested themselves of the *mitsvot*." The reference to their being "little" *(qetannim)* actually refers, not to their physical stature, but to their spiritual condition. They were men of little faith. These people, say the rabbis, were the water carriers of Jericho who had been deprived of their livelihood by Elisha's miracle that made their local brackish water potable.[28] They had no confidence in God's providence, that He would provide them with alternative means of subsistence. They did not call the prophet "baldhead" *(qere'ah)* in reference to his shiny pate, but they said to him, "You have made this place bare for us," that is, "Through you, we lost our means of making a living." In the end, the rabbis make Elisha the guilty one, and he is punished by God for stirring up the bears against the children.

Obviously, this fanciful explanation cannot be defended, but by their wholesale reinterpretation of the narrative, the rabbis of the Talmud actually seem to be passing critical judgment on a particular aspect of biblical morality as reflected in this folk narrative. As Kimhi noted in his comment to 2 Kings 2:24: "They had difficulty in understanding how he (i.e., Elisha) caused their death (i.e., of the children) for such a thing."

A modern scholar might formulate the underlying issue thus: The Hebrew Bible is not a single, uniform, self-consistent system, but is a stratified work, layers of which sometimes represent the imperfect human understanding of the nature of God and His demands on man. That is to say, the written text is not the exclusive source of religious truth, but is, in general, the foundation upon which the edifice of moral truth may be constructed. Such a scholar, depending on his personal commitment, might even say, "the indispensable foundation." However, it is not clear that this formulation would have been acceptable to the rabbis or to the traditional exegetes. Still, rabbinic reinterpretation, or rewriting, of the narratives as described above, raises questions about the authority of the text, the legitimacy of the exegesis, and the relationship between tradition and text.

5. THE HOLISTIC APPROACH

It seems to me that the rabbis, had they been challenged, might have defended their approach on the following grounds: It is the biblical canon in its definitive form that functions as normative. The sacred Scriptures are cumulative in their effect and impact. If the commentators appear to be assuming a stance outside of and over against the text, if they appear to leave room for the play of the intellect and the role of conscience and of moral sensibilities, then it must be appreciated that it is the Hebrew Bible itself in its entirety, as a composite work, that developed and honed these faculties, and that sensitized men to the critical standards to which that same text is now being subjected. The claim is that the commentators are simply actualizing what is potentially there all along, but what is potential can be discerned only through a unitary, comprehensive, holistic approach. This, in fact, is what is partially meant by the rabbinic dictum: "Whatever a mature student may expound in the future, it was already told to Moses on Sinai,"[29] which, incidentally, affords an interesting contrast with the axiom of Pope Stephen I: *Nihil innovetur nisi quod traditum est.*

To return to our point. The classicist, M. I. Finley, noted that the world of the Iliad is saturated with blood because that represented archaic Greek values.[30] We may point out that the Hebrew Scriptures are not saturated with blood and, unlike Homer's role in the world of the Greeks, their morally problematic texts did not, despite constant repetition, promote an inferior code of values. The reason is that the teaching of the text was always accompanied by traditional exegesis which succeeded in transforming that which is time-bound into that which is eternally relevant, and in translating the timelessness of the text into that which is supremely timely. The chronological and cultural gap between the reader and the text was effectively bridged, and the text could and was utilized to mold the mind and to shape the moral character of the Jew.

6. THE PROBLEM OF PESHAṬ

As we have noted, what we have just discussed raises the question of the literal sense of Scripture and its place in the hierarchy of interpretation. There is an interesting exchange on the subject in the works of Maimonides (1135–1204) and Naḥmanides (1194–1270) relative to the Talmudic rule of Shab. 63[a] *et al.* that the text of Scripture may not depart from its straightforward meaning *(peshaṭ)*. In his *Sefer Ha-Mitsvot*,[31] Maimonides states that "there is no Scripture except according to its literal sense" *(peshat),* to which Naḥmanides retorted that the rabbis "did not say that the Bible only has its straightforward meaning, but we have its Midrashic meaning side by side with its straightforward meaning, and the text departs from neither. It can encompass both, and both are the truth; that is to say, the homiletic *(derash)* does not neutralize the literal sense *(peshat)*. Both are substantive."[32]

As R. Loewe and others have shown, what the rabbis meant by *peshat* is less straightforward than meets the eye.[33] What interests me at the moment, however, is the oft-stated proposition that the true and sole task of the biblical scholar is to discover what the contemporary audience understood when the writer wrote what he did, and that such meaning, when recovered, is the one true meaning of the text. Granted, of course, that sound historical research must be the foundation of all biblical scholarship, and that every commentator must commence his exegetical work at that level; but is the interpretation of a text necessarily exhausted by the results of historical investigation, however well based? (In asking this question, I ignore the undeniable fact that there can hardly be a branch of human learning more strewn with the debris of discarded theories than biblical scholarship.)

It seems to me that the rabbis would have held the view that this thesis, taken to its extreme, is of doubtful validity because it is predicated on the presupposition that the biblical writers consciously wrote only for their contemporaries. The rabbis would have said that the internal biblical evidence refutes such a notion and points in the opposite direction, namely that the biblical writers were fully conscious of writing for, and thereby influencing, future generations. Apart from such oft-repeated passages like, "When your son shall ask you in the future, 'What means. . . ?',"[34] and other explicit documentation,[35] the very transmission and survival of the biblical corpus, no less than its astonishing and sustained impact on vast segments of the human race for over two and one half millennia, would be difficult to explain unless the text was very early understood to be proleptic in nature. In other words, the rabbis would have claimed that embedded in the text and context is a deliberate equivocality, the full implication(s) and meaning(s) of which are valid subjects of study by the biblical exegete.

7. MEDIEVAL CRITIQUES OF RABBINIC EXEGESIS

Of course, I am not suggesting that biblical self-understanding always coincides with rabbinic understanding. In fact, as I have elsewhere shown, medieval Jewish exegesis frequently criticizes rabbinic exegesis. Its literature is replete with observations of the most daring kind, much of which well anticipates aspects of modern higher and lower criticism.[36] In fact, the commentators not only may interpret legal or ritual texts not in accord with halakhic ruling, but are quite aware of what they are doing, and sometimes even criticize the rabbinic authorities for divesting the text of its plain meaning. This critical approach constitutes an important element in medieval Jewish exegesis, particularly but not exclusively in the Spanish school, and is not to be viewed as exotic or eccentric though admittedly some of its most extreme expression is both. I should like to emphasize that these scholars were men who were fully committed to the halakhic way of life, and did not question the authority of the rabbis in their legal rulings, only the exegesis by which such were derived from the text. It is almost as though they held—though as far as I know no one has ever articulated it quite this way—that the halakhah enjoys its own autonomous existence and authority, so that the biblical exegete is free to investigate the text independently of dogmatic or traditional considerations.

By way of illustration, I might point to Rashi's rejection of the tannaitic exegesis of Exod. 23:2. There Scripture states: "You shall not side with the mighty to do wrong—you shall not give perverse testimony in a dispute so as to pervert it in favor of the mighty." The Mishnah understands this verse to require a simple majority of judges for an acquittal but a majority of two for a conviction in capital cases.[37] On this Rashi comments, "There are interpretations of this verse by the sages of Israel, but the language of the text cannot accommodate them." Rashi's grandson, known as RashBaM (ca. 1080–1158), in discussing the rabbinic exposition of Lev. 7:18 as found in M. Zev 2:2–4, T.B. Zev 29[b], asserts that "The sages have wrested it from its plain meaning." Perhaps the most forthright expression of the independence of medieval Jewish exegesis from tradition is to be found in an observation by Samuel b. Hofni, Gaon of Sura (d. 1030), cited by David Kimhi in his comment to 1 Sam. 28:24: "Even though the words of the sages in the Talmud imply that the woman (the witch of Endor) really did revive Samuel, yet insofar as human reason rejects this, they cannot be accepted."

In the same strain, we may cite the comments of Isaac Abravanel (1437–1508) in connection with the narrative of 2 Sam. 11–12. In the Talmud,[38] it is related that the 3rd–4th century C.E. Palestinian Amora R. Samuel ben Nahman, citing R. Jonathan ben Eleazar (3rd century C.E.) as his source, exonerated David from any sin. This is achieved by means of contortive exegesis in plain defiance of the straightforward intent of the text, the Prophet Nathan's severe castigation of David's shameful conduct, David's self-confession of his guilt, and the tradition reflected in Ps. 51. Although most of the medieval commentators follow the talmudic rationale, Abravanel launches into a blistering indictment of David, probingly analyzing the multiple sins that the king committed. He does this in full and open consciousness of his contradiction of the talmudic exegesis which he describes as being contrary to "the simple truth."

The kind of freedom and intellectual honesty that such comments, and many more like them, display clearly points to a separation of matters of faith and law from matters of scholarship on the part of these medievals, a distinction that, alas, is often blurred today. Put another way, these traditional Jewish exegetes are really operating according to rabbinic doctrine that the oral Torah, the *torah she-be'al peh*, codified as Halakhah, is one of the two modes of God's self-revelation to Israel, and the process of continuous reinterpretation and adaptation of the Halakhah to new and everchanging conditions is affected by the indwelling of the Divine Presence in those whose piety, learning and acknowledged authority are such as to give normative force to their halakhic decisions. Where the exegetes assert their intellectual independence is, first, in respect of the humanly wrought exegetical process by which the oral Torah is interlaced with the written Torah, *torah she-bikhtav,* and, second, in the exposition of the non-halakhic sections of the Bible.

NOTES

1. Tosef. Shab. 13:1.
2. Gershom Scholem, *The Messianic Idea in Judaism* (New York, 1971), p. 290.
3. See S. Rawidowicz. "On Interpretation" in *Studies in Jewish Thought,* Philadelphia, 1974, pp. 45–80.
4. TB *Sanh.* 34ª, cf. *Shab.* 88ᵇ.
5. Num.R. *Naso',* 13:15.
6. M. *Avot* 5:26.
7. See A. I. Baumgarten, "Justinian and the Jews" in *Rabbi Joseph H. Lookstein Memorial Volume,* ed. Leo Landman (New York, 1980), pp. 37–44.
8. On Ben Hayyim's Rabbinic Bible, see now Jordan S. Penkover, *Jacob ben Hayyim and the Rise of the Biblia Rabbanica* [Hebrew], Hebrew University Doctoral Dissertation, Jerusalem, 1982.
9. TB *Erubin* 13ᵇ.
10. See J. A. Sanders, *Torah and Canon* (Philadelphia, 1972); *idem,* "Available for Life: The Nature and Function of Canon" in *Magnalia Dei: Essays on the Bible and Archaeology in Memory of G. Ernest Wright* (New York, 1976), pp. 531–60; B. S. Childs, *The Introduction to the Old Testament as Scripture* (Philadelphia, 1979); J. Barr, *Holy Scripture: Canon, Authority, Criticism* (Philadelphia, 1983); M. Fishbane, *Biblical Interpretation in Ancient Israel* (Oxford, 1984).
11. Cf. N. M. Sarna, "Ps. 89: A Study in Inner Biblical Exegesis," in *Biblical and Other Studies,* ed. A. Altmann, Philip W. Lown Institute of Advanced Judaic Studies, Brandeis University, Studies and Texts, Vol. I (Cambridge, 1963), pp. 29–46.
12. 2 Chron. 36:23.
13. Exod. 34:13; Deut. 12:2–3.

14. Deut. 16:21.

15. Cf. 1 Kings 14:23; Jer. 2:20; Ezek. 6:13.

16. Cf. *špš 'lm* in U. T. 2008:7 and *rpu mlk 'lm* in U. T. 52.1 on which see M. Pope, *BASOR*, 251 (1983), p. 68; cf. F. M. Cross, *Canaanite Myth and Hebrew Epic* (Cambridge, 1973), pp. 17, n. 29; 18 and n. 33.

17. Cf. Gen. 12:8; 13:4; 26:25.

18. So *Gen. R.* 54.7.

19. *pundok* = Gr. *pandocheion*.

20. So Rashi to TB *Sotah* 10[a].

21. Cf. Gen. 6:3.

22. TB *Sanh.* 108[a-b]

23. *Gen. R.* 32:9.

24. S. R. Driver, *Genesis*, Westminster Commentaries (London, 1904), *ad loc.*

25. H. E. Ryle, *The Book of Genesis*, Cambridge Bible (Cambridge, 1921), *ad loc.*

26 J. Skinner, *Genesis*, International Critical Commentary (Edinburgh, 1910), *ad loc.*

27. TB *Sotah* 46[a]–47[b].

28. 2 Kings 2:19–25.

29. *P. Peah* 2:4 *et al.* See A. J. Heschel, *Torah Min Ha-Shamayim* (London-New York, 1965), Vol. 2, p. 236 and n. 10.

30. *The World of Odysseus* (New York, 1959), p. 127.

31. ed. Ch. Heller, Vol. II (Jerusalem-New York, 1976), pp. 7–8.

32. *Hassagot Ha-RaMBaN* II, p. 27.

33. See R. Loewe, *Papers of the Institute of Jewish Studies* I, ed. J. G. Weiss (Jerusalem, 1964), pp. 140–185; cf. B. S. Childs, "The Sensus Literalis of Scripture: An Ancient and Modern Problem," in *Beiträge zur Alttestamentlichen Theologie, Festschrift für Walther Zimmerli zum 70 Geburtstag* (Göttingen, 1977), pp. 80–93; M. Schneiders, "Faith, Hermeneutics and the Literal Sense of Scripture," in *Theological Studies*, 39 (1978), pp. 719–736.

34. Exod. 13:14, cf. v. 8; Deut. 6:8; Josh. 4:6, 21; 22:27–28, cf. v. 24.

35. Cf. Isa. 30:8; Jer. 30:2–3; 36:28–29; Dan. 12:4.

36. "Hebrew and Biblical Studies in Medieval Spain," in *The Sephardi Heritage*, ed. R. Barnett (London, 1971), pp. 344–394; "Unusual Aspects of Medieval Biblical Exegesis" [Hebrew] in *Thought and Action: Essays in Memory of Simon Rawidowicz on the Twenty-fifth Anniversary of His Death*, ed. A. A. Greenbaum and A. L. Ivry (Tel Aviv, 1983), pp. 35–42; "The Modern Study of the Bible in the Framework of Jewish Studies," in *Proceedings of the Eighth World Congress of Jewish Studies: Bible and Hebrew Language* (Jerusalem, 1983), pp. 19–27.

37. *M. Sanh.* 1:6.

38. TB *Shab.* 56[a].

The Role of Tradition
in the Reading of Scripture

Jorge Mejia

One of the major issues to be faced by Christians and Jews is how Scripture should be read, interpreted and, eventually, applied to our own lives, individual of course, but in the first place communitarian. Such issue affects both great religious traditions, Judaism and Christianity, which look to Scripture as their *norma normans*.

I. HOW TO READ SCRIPTURE

It is well known to Christian and Catholic scholars at large how dramatically this last question has divided Christianity for almost four hundred years, since the Reformation. It is also well known how the Second Vatican Council has decisively contributed to the solution of the internal Christian debate by affirming in its Dogmatic Constitution *Dei Verbum* (n. 9):

> Sacred Tradition and sacred Scripture, then, are bound closely together, and communicate one with the other. For both of them, flowing out from the same divine well-spring, come together in some fashion to form one thing, and move toward the same goal.

And the following reason is given for such intimate relationship:

> Sacred Scripture is the *speech of God* as it is put down in writing under the breath of the Holy Spirit. And Tradition transmits in its entirety the *Word of God* which has been entrusted to the apostles by Christ the Lord and the Holy Spirit. It transmits it to the successors of the apostles . . . (*ibid.*, itals. mine).

21

It is thus clear, either from the last paragraph quoted, or from what precedes the first quoted statement in n. 8, that the relationship between Tradition
and Scripture, for the Council, consists in the fact that Scripture is "the word
of God" *(locutio Dei)* in writing, while Tradition transmits (or communicates)
"the same word of God" *(verbum Dei)*. As the word of God is only *one*, it is
easy to understand why the Council teaches that "both of them, flow out from
the same well-spring" (n. 9). Both come, in final analysis, from God, revealing Himself to humanity, through the Patriarchs, the Prophets, the Sages,
and Christ.

If in this pregnant formulation the solution can be found to the internal
Christian debate (and as a matter of fact the relation between Scripture and
Tradition is *not* on the agenda of any of the present major ecumenical dialogues
of which the Roman Catholic Church is part), this does not mean that thereby
all the problems created by the relation just mentioned are automatically
solved. One can however argue that the principles stated by the Council may
help toward the solution also of newer and different albeit connected problems.
This holds true, of course, first and foremost, of a solution valid for the Catholic Church, to whom the Council documents are addressed. But it is to be
hoped that the consideration of the principles referred to might also be prof-
itable to Judaism.

(a) Exegetical Methods

The new problem with which we are all faced presently can be boldly
stated in these terms: Is Scripture to be read *critically* or *traditionally*, namely
in the (normative) light of a religious tradition?

The problem is, of course, not *that* new. It was at least implicit in the
acrimonious debate in the Catholic Church around the turn of this century
about what was then held to be a "modernistic" interpretation of Scripture.[1]
On the one hand, the debate then was perceived and lived through as one more
instance of the larger debate between "Faith and Science," and on the other
(and for the same reason) it was ideologized right from the start and thus the
philosophical issues soon became predominant, thereby obscuring the proper
biblical issues.[2] The result was that historico-critical exegesis (as it was already
called)[3] was looked upon with mistrust and distaste in the Catholic Church and
had to wait till "Divino Afflante Spiritu" (30 Sept. 1943)[4] to see its proper
place acknowledged in Catholic Bible study. The Council thereafter ratified
Pius XII's teaching in the Encyclical (cf. *Dei Verbum*, n. 12).

In the meantime, however, and much more acutely since then, the proper
criteria for the reading and interpretation of Scripture in the Church, and their

proper application, have been the subject of much discussion and, even more, of conflicting not to say contradictory use.[5]

The question stated in more precise terms is this: Are historico-critical methods to be taken as the last absolute instance for the interpretation of Scripture, in the sense that, if conclusions arrived at thanks to the application of such methods run counter to the traditional teaching of the Church, this is to be either abandoned or radically changed?

Let me try to refine still more the formulation of the question at issue. It is not that some isolated text (or texts) of Scripture, in which a particular doctrine has been traditionally seen to find its "proof," is now demonstrated on critical grounds, not to be able to carry such burden anymore. This, in fact, is not *at all* the problem.

In the first place, it must be granted that to put too much weight on any particular text to "prove" a certain doctrine is both unwise and dangerous.[6] It can therefore be helpful and healthy to have such text or texts critically examined and perhaps removed from their unique position.

Then, the question is again *not* the use of historico-critical methods in themselves, in the large and variegated gamut of the present array of such methods,[7] but their proper place in the interpretation of Scripture. Is this to be *final, decisive* and self-sufficient, so as to render superfluous and vain any other way of assessing the sense of the Bible?

Or perhaps better still: Is the true sense of Holy Scripture fully attainable *only* through historico-critical methods? What happens then when conflicts arise and, for instance, not any "proof" text, but a whole essential Christian doctrine, like the redemptive value of the death of Christ, is held to be a late *theologumenon* belonging to more recent strata in the New Testament, completely alien to the historical truth of the life and death of Jesus, as far at least as those can be the object of proper historical knowledge?

This would be, in fact, the conclusion of a series of critical analyses, ranging from the literary criticism of the present text of the Gospels to the following up of the history of the tradition of the substitutive or redemptive death to the examination of the different "Sitze im Leben der Gemeinde" where such a tradition might have had its birthplace.

If this is but one example, it is indeed an outstanding one.[8] However, particular examples are not much to the point, the main question being how Scripture is to be approached, read, interpreted and, therefore, preached and applied. And this raises the whole problematic of Tradition.

How are we to deal with such a problem which, I believe, is rapidly becoming the major problem in the field of Christian (not only Catholic) access to Holy Scripture?

The first thing to be said, most emphatically, is that historico-critical methods are here to stay and that it is useless, nay dangerous, to ignore them or deny their proper value.[9] I would go still further and say that I am personally convinced that the discovery and pertinent refining of such methods (which are not at all finished, as I shall add in a moment) are a gift of grace of the Lord of Scripture to His Church, or more comprehensively to those, in any religious tradition dependent on the Bible, dedicated to its study. So, from whichever side, historico-critical methods should be received not only with tolerance and resignation, like unavoidable evil, but as a positive good.[10] This means, in its turn, that one has to appreciate and highly respect such methods, being always open to the results of their proper and adequate application.

With this goes hand in hand—because it is also a form of respect—a real care not to use those methods (or have others use them) to "prove" our traditional tenets. This, in fact, can only obscure the issues and will, in final analysis, do more harm than good.[11] The whole point is precisely that truly traditional doctrine is not "proved" nor, on the other hand, "disproved" by critical analyses, however much its scriptural basis can be refined or purified through the use of such methods.

Methods, then, are not in themselves absolute nor infallible. The very fact that so many and varied have emerged in the last one hundred years, from Abraham Kuenen's and Julius Wellhausen's *Quellenkritik* up to F. Bovon's structural analysis and beyond, is in itself a call to moderation and relativization. Not any one method is in itself sufficient—therefore, not even all taken together, not as we know them now or, for that matter, at any time in the future.[12]

Reflection on the methods is in order—not only, I would insist, on their proper scientific characteristics and appropriate ways of application in themselves and in relation to each other (a reflection which, I fear, is yet to be done), but much more on their intrinsic limitations *as* methods, seen in a proper historical perspective.

(b) Imponderables of Exegesis

Such reflection might perhaps be helped by some or all of the following considerations. We are not to feel that, whatever merits present methods may have brought with them, what was done before, in the long history of Christian (and, of course, Jewish) exegesis, is altogether expendable. Patristic, medieval and Reform/Counterreform exegesis had its limits, no doubt. But the whole point is whether it only had limitations or, rather, whether those limitations were in fact the outer face of a very positive and enriching exegetical work, truly conducive to the discovery of the sense of Scripture.[13]

The same can be foreseen, with no excessive effort of our imagination, of any new methods apt to be devised in the future.

This leads me to a deeper consideration. I have said above that no method is self-sufficient, nor all taken together. I would now add that not any method, nor any amount of methods, can appropriately exhaust *the sense* embedded in any writing.

Such affirmation, I believe, is not new and should not really upset anybody. It means at least two things: first, that whatever a human writer intends to put into writing, if it truly expresses his/her mind, it is, properly speaking, unfathomable, no mind being entirely equal to any other mind, and writing being, at its best, an inadequate instrument of expression. Second, precisely because of this, written texts have a life of their own, to a certain extent independent of whoever wrote them down first, and dependent, on the other hand, on the process of transmission of such texts in a given milieu, society, or religious community.

This means, if I am not mistaken, that it is not only the remoteness of origin, the long-lost cultural environment, the foreign (perhaps dead) language in which it is couched, or the anonymity of the writer, which makes a written text difficult to interpret. It is *the text* itself,[14] however much the above mentioned circumstances may add to it. But, on the other hand, that which helps toward the adequate reading of the text in question, besides and beyond the interpretive methods applied during a certain segment of time, is the living history of the text, authoritative religious reading included (if the case may be) and most certainly older commentaries, practical applications and other uses to which it may be put. This is why Tradition is so necessary for the reading of Holy Scripture and why also historico-critical methods appear intrinsically limited.

Further, whoever uses or applies historico-critical methods to a text must also reflect very carefully on the ideological/philosophical presuppositions, either carried by such methods or alive in one's own mind, or both, because there *are* philosophical implications and one can only ignore them at one's own peril. It is not at all the same to try to rearrange the different redactional strata of a given Gospel with the ingrained conviction (conscious or unconscious) that what really happened in Palestine around the year 30 of the first century CE with a certain man called Jesus cannot be known nor does it matter very much anyway whether it is known or not, or to start the same process with a different conviction, namely that one can at least arrive at *some* adequate knowledge of what happened to that man, through the texts proposed to our analysis, and indeed that such knowledge is supremely important.

Thus, the philosophical and theological questions cannot but be posed, in the process itself of the exegetical task.[15]

There is no denying the fact that we *all* have philosophico-theological presuppositions. On the contrary, this must be affirmed, not as if it were a kind of regrettable human limitation, as if the hypothetic ideal was the absence of such presuppositions *(tamquam tabula rasa)*. I very much fear that such a conception is in itself an unfortunate philosophical (or pseudo-philosophical) inheritance. The human mind approaches its object prepared in a certain way by education, culture, sociological and ideological contexts, and indeed deep personal and religious commitments. This *does not* prevent it from appropriately reading its object—the text, in our case. On the contrary, it is certainly helpful if, on the one hand, the subject is made conscious of such presuppositions and, on the other hand, if some or all of them belong to the same sphere of being or reality to which the object belongs. Critically reading a religious text with an a-religious mind may be perhaps an interesting exercise in intellectual curiosity, not however the true way of finding the clue to the text's proper interpretation. Here again we seem to be beyond the realm of historico-critical methods.

To become conscious of one's own presuppositions implies also to accept (or reject) them as part and parcel of the intellectual panoply of the subject. This further means that philosophical presuppositions have to be sorted out and discussed, the more so when they are not a definite personal position but just an element of the cultural climate of a given period, place or category of "experts." Thus, not all exegetes may have perhaps solid personal convictions about either the unknowability of reality, static or dynamic, or about the possibility of change in nature or natural phenomena. But, in a certain intellectual climate, the negative conclusions about both such philosophical problems may have become part of the common heritage. They are not discussed anymore. I would say that such are precisely the presuppositions to be discussed. Otherwise, the exegetical enterprise will be slanted in a certain way, opposed, I would presume, to what the writers of the books or texts we examine spontaneously do believe. In this sense, a process of "demythologizing" applied to such writings would only amount to the suppression of whatever constitutes the canvas on which their message rests.[16] The message itself would then fall to pieces.

(c) Exegesis and Faith

All this, however, is not sufficient. Specifically religious writings, like Sacred Scripture, are not adequately understood only and when philosophical questions are solved. We are not criticizing a certain temptation of absoluteness on behalf of the historico-critical methods, only to affirm *next* the absoluteness of valid philosophical conclusions.

There is, however, a certain difference between one and the other. Methods are only methods, important and necessary as they may be. What is essential with them is the way in which they are used and the fundamental orientation they receive from the presuppositions governing their use. These last become, then, decisive.

Yet, they are not enough. The "Spirit" which inspired Scripture is the Spirit *of God,* and it is under this Spirit that we are supposed to read and interpret it.[17] This means, at the very least, that *faith* is the proper presupposition to understand the Bible.

Does this mean that outside the faith commitment there is no way to arrive at any truth in Scripture? Or that historico-critical methods, used outside the pale of faith, will only and necessarily arrive at wrong conclusions?

This is a preposterous affirmation and I, for one, would never subscribe to it. I insist also that it is in no way implied by what I am now trying to say. The whole question is much more complicated and requires delicate nuancing.

There is no denying that historico-critical methods (very much like scientific ones, which they approach), properly applied, can and should arrive at sure, valid conclusions. This is why I said above that their discovery or refinement is a gift of God. Human reason is, in fact, a gift of God. And this should never be forgotten if we do not want to fall into a kind of irrational fideism. As I shall say in a moment, even our most cherished religious traditions, at whose light we read the Bible, are to be scrutinized by reason.

The sense, therefore, of the above affirmation is not that the exegete has to choose between critical methods and reading in faith. Such antithesis would be radically opposite to Catholic Tradition, witness "Divino Afflante Spiritu," explicitly written to counter such extreme positions.[18]

It is not a question of either/or. It is a question of respecting and accepting the true status of Scripture as the Word of God, conveying through human expression, with all its inherent ambiguity, true revelation.

How does one perceive the Word or receive the revelation without first turning in humble obedience and total commitment to the One who speaks and reveals, which means exactly "to believe," *he' emîn, pisteuein*?

As the revealing Word is couched in human terms, not above or to the side of them, rational methods of analysis, in an appropriate philosophical climate, are required to discern the exact value of each term, and of all taken together. This, however, is not the fullness of the message, which is proclaimed not only to enlighten the mind but to kindle the heart and, in the final analysis, to transform our lives. When Scripture is not read in this way, one cannot help but be reminded of the severe judgment of one of the ancient Church Fathers: "corticem rodunt, medullam non attingunt" (Hyer. epist. 98 ad Paulinum, 9, 1, CSEL 54, 538). And it could be added that what really gives justification to the use of the critical methods is that they help us break the "cortex" of the fruit so as to taste the substance.[19]

The Spirit, then, with which Scripture must be read, written with a capital S, is, as we have said, the Spirit of God—the Spirit which dwells and works or operates in every believer, great or small, and in the whole Church.

But the argument can also be enlarged, and thereby made to affirm that even if we write the word "spirit" with a minuscule, the axiom would still be true. Because it is the "spirit" of a written text, its "soul," so to speak, the intimate inspiration or source from which it proceeds and on which it lives its life, temporal and transient, or eternal, and imperishable, that constitutes the only true clue for its adequate interpretation—a spirit (if not *the* Spirit) which has to be discovered, caught and made his/her own by the reader or the exegete, beyond and above all the critical methods he/she is wont to use. This is true of any writing worth its name. It is eminently true of the Sacred Writing which we venerate, Holy Scripture. In such a way, a certain "connaturality" with the writing we examine seems to be required for its adequate understanding, meaning by this the access to the message it conveys in itself and in its traditional reading.

Therefore, the true *sense* of Scripture, meaning by this the revealed and operative truth of its message, is only to be discovered in faith, however much the critical methods can and should help toward its attainment. But it certainly goes beyond them and nobody should be shocked if the affirmations or conclusions of the one and the other do not always coincide.

II. CONSISTENCY OF EXEGESIS

The Tradition of the Church has made its own reading of Scripture, expressed in the commentaries and preaching of the Fathers, in the teaching of the Councils, in the doctrinal statements of other instances in the Church, and in the generalized faith conviction of the Christian community ("sensus fidei"). Such reading, of which one could give many examples, is simultaneously dependent and independent of the various critical methods applied to the study of Scripture along the ages.

It is *dependent* on them, because it has always to be critically, that is rationally, grounded and assessed, and thus able to be proved to whoever "asks the reason for this hope" of ours (cf. 1 Pt 3:16). The means of proof will not always be the same, and we shall be brought to drop some and look for others along history. This is what historico-critical methods are for, and why they have to be used and constantly refined.

But it is also *independent,* because the truth it discovers and conveys is not as such subject to the changing modes and occasional prerogatives of any method. It finds namely its source only in the Spirit which wrote Scripture and teaches the Church how to read it: "He will guide you to all truth" (John 16:13).

The proper consequence is, I believe, that the reading of Scripture by the Church has a consistency of its own and is not to be dismissed if, at least apparently, the use of critical methods arrives at different conclusions. It would not however be a "different" conclusion, in the sense of opposite to the former or incompatible with it, because this one belongs to another realm of human knowledge, a realm, I would say, that is above and beyond the field attained by critical scientific methods. The structure of reality and the corresponding structure of knowing should be recognized and respected.

On the other hand, this implies that the *expression* of the truth belonging to Tradition and found in Scripture, its place in the Sacred Writings, its connection with other truths of the same category and, generally speaking, the synthesis of which it is a part must be constantly submitted to careful scrutiny and critique in the light of the conclusions arrived at through the use of historico-critical methods. But it would be giving to those methods more weight than they can carry, to hold their conclusions to be infallible, in any given segment of time. As I said above, they (and their conclusions) are to be constantly and strictly criticized, renewed and replaced in a different synthesis. For this, the critical exegete has to be a good critic, but if he/she is to understand at all the main dimension of the task, he/she is to be primarily a person of faith, namely somebody attuned to God speaking to reveal Himself in Scripture and actively conscious of his/her belonging to a religious traditional community, created by Scripture and whence, in the first place, Scripture came into being. Thus he/she will avoid the inner contradiction in life and in work, which instead will beset him/her if, by pretending to serve and understand Scripture, such a person tries to stand outside Tradition. The only way, in fact, truly to serve and understand Scripture is to receive it *from* Tradition, and to hand it on *inside* the same Tradition.

(a) Inferences for Christian Exegesis

Some conclusions can be drawn, I believe, from the above exposition, which will help toward proper understanding and avoid confusion.

The *first* is that any human text cannot be thoroughly and completely understood in all the dimensions of the sense[20] it carries, through literary or critical means alone.

Second, this inherent sense comes of course from the writer but goes beyond the means of expression he used, and relates also to the text itself as an independent entity and to the reading of it in its transmission. This is why no commentary (for instance, of the *Divina Commedia*) is, or will be, final.

Third, a text held to be of divine origin, although written with human means, is not in itself a *monstrum,* but requires a very precise methodology of interpretation (or hermeneutics). It is to be studied critically, but it should be clear from the start that whatever lies hidden in its pages will never be accessible by such means only.

Fourth, the reason for this is not only the inexhaustible richness of any human text, but also, and indeed in the first place, its transcendent character, so to speak, namely the fact that God speaks through it for the salvation of human beings.

Fifth, faith is therefore the proper clue of interpretation, not only as an individual act of knowledge, but also as the way of entering into the community which properly ''bears'' the book and to whom it speaks in the first place, and God through it.

Sixth, even this reading in faith, helped and controlled (in a way) by the application of critical methods, is not final, in the sense that there will always be a deepening of understanding and a new discovery of sense with new possibilities and forms of application of the text to our lives.

Seventh, this does not mean necessarily that there are two kinds of truths, or two unconnected realms of knowledge, but it does mean that reality, or rather the reality of the sense of words, lies deeper than our means can fathom, and infinitely so when the word in question comes from God.[21]

b) *Judaism and Scripture*

The horizon of the preceding presentation is obviously Christian, and more specifically Catholic. Here and there, however, some allusion has been made to Judaism, in relation to the same problematic of Bible and Tradition. Judaism is, in fact, a religion ''of the Bible,'' however much it leans to acts, and the following of a ''way'' *(halakha).*

It would not be proper for me to dwell at length on the specific Jewish aspects of the above described problematic—nor would I be, I fear, up to the task.

Nevertheless, I venture here to suggest two possible foci of interest in such a problematic for Christians interested in Judaism.

The *first* aspect I would like to underline in present day Judaism and its very alive concern with Holy Scripture is the wide chasm, at least to an outsider, which seems to be open still between religious Bible study (in the Yeshivot, for instance) and the use of historico-critical methods. In other words, the existing chasm between scientific Bible study and Tradition.

It is significant, in this connection, to register the fact that in the Hebrew University in Jerusalem Bible studies are pursued, and indeed at the highest scientific level, in the Department of Letters and Philosophy. In the same vein, in the series of remarkable World Congresses of Sciences of Judaism, held in the same venue, representatives of Jewish traditional Bible study are conspicuously absent. Nobody, I would say, among the non-Jewish participants is particularly happy with such absence.

(c) Dialogue and Exegesis

That the dialogue between both tendencies is not impossible, men like Umberto Cassuto in the past, Nahum Sarna and Jonah Greenfield in this time (and, of course, Jacob Neusner in his own field) are there to prove. One would hope that this dialogue would be continued, enlarged and deepened. All of us, in the Christian scholarly world of Bible studies, will have much to reap from it.

Secondly, and more perhaps to the point, the relation of normative Rabbinical tradition *(Torah She be 'alPeh)* and Scripture *(Torah She-bikhtav)* poses a series of strong challenges to the religiously minded Christian Bible scholar.

On the one hand, both Torot seem to run parallel from Moses down to the men of the Great Synagogue (*Avoth* 1,1; Danby's translation) and beyond. From this point of view, the relation between Scripture and Tradition would seem limited to the common source, divine (The Lord) and human (Moses). On the other hand, there is a definite intention, at least in large segments of the normative Rabbinical Tradition, to base one Torah on the other or rather to bring it forth from it. This is, if I am not entirely mistaken, the meaning and function of the *middot,* either the seven of Hillel, or the thirteen of Rabbi Ishmael, or the thirty-two of Eliezer ben Jose ha gelili.[22] The "pillar" on which such hermeneutics rest is, in the first place, the unity of the Bible, a cardinal principle of traditional Christian hermeneutics,[23] and, further, "the unity of written and oral law."[24] There is much to be learned from this remarkable insistence on linking one Torah with the other, and both with God's original revelation.[25]

The place of historico-critical methods in this hermeneutic position remains, I believe, to be worked out. Or perhaps—and this would be the more radical challenge of all—no place is found for it at all.

It remains to be underlined again that what gives to Scripture its peculiarity, indeed its absolutely unique status, both in Jewish and Christian tradition, is that it comes from God—and this is an article of faith. To "come from God" means here that the divine voice resounds *presently* in Scripture and that the divine mind is *presently* made open to us through its words. Such is the teaching of Tradition.

It is easy to see what a unique challenge this poses for the application to the study of Scripture of any human methods of analysis. It means, in final resolve, the meeting of the divine and the human, which is precisely the mystery of Scripture itself and, in the specifically Christian profession of faith, the mystery of Christ.[26]

NOTES

1. The original French expression is "modernisme."
2. Cf. the title of one of the last works of A. Loisy, the main French representative of "modernisme": *La Religion de l'Avenir*. Both the Holy Office Decree "Lamentabili sane exitu" (3 July 1907) and the almost immediately following (8 September 1907) Encyclical Letter "Pascendi dominici gregis" of Pius X are witnesses to the philosophical content of Modernism (the Decree in its entirety and large extracts of the Encyclical Letter can be read in Denz.-Schön, *Enchiridion*, ed. XXXIV, nn. 3401 to 3466 and 3475 to 3500).
3. Cf. Fr. M.J. Lagrange's book entitled *La Méthode historique* (Paris, 1905). Fr. Lagrange was among the founding scholars of the Ecole Biblique et Archéologique Française de Jérusalem, now quickly approaching its centenary.
4. The Encyclical Letter, beginning with these words was published by Pius XII in the midst of a very harsh controversy provoked by an attack against the way historico-critical methods were applied in Catholic biblical teaching and in higher Catholic institutions of biblical scholarship, like the Pontifical Biblical Institute in Rome—an attack, which, sad to say, was repeated almost identically twenty years later at the opening of the Second Vatican Council.
5. There exists a rather long bibliography on the subject, which I do not intend to list here. I limit myself to my own article: "A Christian View of Bible Interpretation," *Biblical Studies: Meeting Ground of Jews and Christians*. Boadt, Croner, Klenicki, eds. A Stimulus Book (New York: Paulist Press, 1980, pp. 45–72) and the articles of Fr. Dreyfus quoted there in n.65. To this I would now add Ignace de la Potterie, "Esegesi storico-critica e interpretazione cristiana. L'esegesi cattolica oggi," in *Parola e Spirito* (Studi in onore di Settimio Cipriani, Brescia, Paideia editrice s.d.), pp. 3–10; Raymond E. Brown, *The Critical Meaning of the Bible* (New York: Paulist Press, 1981) with the bibliographical note I published in *L'Osservatore Romano* (7–8 June 1982)

under the title: "Un recente studio sul senso 'critico' della Bibbia''; M. Hengel, *Acts and the History of Earliest Christianity* (Philadelphia: Fortress Press, 1980) Part III, "Historical Methods and the Theological Interpretation of the New Testament," pp. 129–136. I would like to quote here the relevant sentences in the Preface of Hengel's book (pp. vii-viii): "Two things, above all, concern me. First, to question the radical historical skepticism which is so widespread in a number of areas within German scholarship; this skepticism is often coupled with flights of imagination which suggest a retreat from any historical research worth taking seriously. Second, however, I am no less vigorously opposed to the primitive ostracism of historical—and that always means critical—methods without which neither historical nor theological understanding of the New Testament is possible. It is remarkable how closely the two extremes can converge in this 'flight from history,' no matter what the reasons for it may be." I couldn't agree more with the opinions here expressed.

6. This is in no way intended to detract the "special status" of some scriptural texts in Catholic tradition. It is apt to note in this connection that such texts are, first, *pauci* (but a few), as "Divino afflante" states (*Ench. biblicum*, Naples-Rome 1954, n. 565; the latter sentence uses the neuter plural *pauca*), and then they can always be the subject of more and renewed study, which will help understand them better in themselves and in a deeper synthesis.

7. Attention is to be paid, however, to the relative value and rational cumulative application of the different methods, and therefore not to unduly privilege one above others (like the source-critical method in the past, the *form-geschichtliche* method now and, in other circles, structuralism).

8. There have been *three* recent critical studies on this problem, all from the German exegetical community: M. Schürmann, *Comment Jésus a-t-il vécu sa mort?* (Paris: Les Editions du Cerf, 1977; German original: 1975), pp. 57–66, 67–68, etc.; M. Hengel, *La Crucifixion* (ib. 1981); (this French edition is very much enlarged in relation to the German original, included in E. Käsemann's *Festschrift*, published in 1976), especially the Deuxième partie: La mort expiatoire de Jésus par "substitution" (pp. 117–203); Peter Stuhlmacher, "Existenzstellvertretung für die Vielen: Mk. 10,45 (Mt. 20,28)," in *Versöhnung, Gesetz und Gerechtigkeit, Aufsätze zur biblischen Theologie* (Göttingen: Vandenhoeck und Ruprecht, 1981), pp. 27–42 (first published in Claus Westermann's *Festschrift*, in 1980).

9. Cf. the quotation from M. Hengel's Preface to *Acts and the History of Early Christianity* in note 5 above.

10. Cf. Hengel (note 5 above) p. 132: 3.1.3: "the constant expansion, control and correction of the historical 'consciousness' is in principle to be affirmed as a 'good work' of discovering truth''; p. 134: 4.2 " 'Theological exegesis,' which thinks that it can 'interpret' the New Testament without the application of the relevant historical methods, is not only deaf to the question of truth but is also in danger of distorting what the texts say and falling victim to docetic speculation".

11. Cf. ib. p.132: 2.4.4. "Historical research . . . cannot provide a basis for the truth-claim of theology. . . ." This is the inherent mistake of all fundamentalism, and

it has particularly misused archeology for "proving" the truth of biblical history and theology, almost since the beginning of systematic archeological investigation, from Sir Charles Warren's book down to Werner Keller's *Die Bibel hat doch Recht.* Both archeology and theology have suffered from such misuse.

12. Cf. again Hengel's thesis, *ubi supra* (p. 129): 1.1 "Talk about 'the historical critical method' is questionable"; 1.1.1 "In reality there is a variety of historical methods"; 1.1.3 "Historical research must always remain open to the testing of new methods," etc.

13. One can glean from de la Potterie's article quoted in note 5 some principles inspiring Patristic exegesis: "Per Ireneo e per Cirillo Alessandrino, il versetto di Gv.1.14 sul'Verbo fatto carne' non riguarda solo il mistero di Cristo; contiene in ugual misura una importante norma per l'interpretazione della *Scrittura.* La realtà della Incarnazione si prolunga e si dispiega nell'esegesi ecclesiale . . . dobbiamo leggere nella Scrittura una serie di eventi storici ed umani, ma anche l'economia della revelazione e della salvezza . . ." (p. 8). "Un altro principio che ritorna di frequente presso i Padri è espresso dall'aforismo 'uno solo e il medesimo' *(eîs kaî autós)"* (ib.). One could easily list another, even more basic principle, like the conviction that Scripture is at the same time, and indivisively, divine and human, exactly like Jesus Christ.

14. Modern hermeneutics, on one side, and structuralism, on the other, have insisted strongly on the very special status of the text as such. But without at all detracting from the attention given in recent research to the written text, it is only fair to recall that patristic and medieval exegetical analysis have always considered the inspired text of the Bible as a kind of independent entity, with its own internal system of norms, correlations and meanings. If, then, the axiom "optima exegesis quid senscrit auctor" is not at all a recent discovery in Christian exegesis (cf. vgr. S.Theol. I,1,10: "sensus litteralis est quem auctor intendit"), it seems quite true to say that the emphasis laid on such exegetic principle in the last century or so has done much to obscure the unique importance of the text as such. Most of this applies also to Jewish exegesis.

15. It is most remarkable that for the Jerusalem Symposium *de interrelatione evangeliorum,* April 1983, the organizers had already included in the program a certain number of lectures on the traditional and even philosophical aspects of the critical problem central to the discussion: the Synoptic question. I am convinced however that the turn the debate took especially during the second week, clearly demonstrated that, while historico-critical methods are altogether needed for the solution of what is in itself a critical problem, the problem as such raises a much larger and deeper series of questions, which cannot be possibly avoided at one or the other stage of the discussion.

16. It is obvious that the question here is not "above" or "below," or the appearances of cosmic phenomena. This is not the *canvas* of the message, although it may be part of the mold of its expression. The reality of God, of His purpose upon man and world, of His lordship over nature and history, the possibility of His communication with us through inspiration and revelation—this (and several other things) are the *canvas* referred to in the text.

17. This axiom has been lately repeated in the Dogmatic Constitution *Dei Ver-*

bum of the Second Vatican Council, precisely in the section on Catholic hermeneutics (n. 12). It is there properly referred to Hyeronemus, *in Gal.* 5, 19–21 (PL 26, 417A), where the text reads "(Scripturam esse legendam et interpretandam non aliter) quam sensus Spiritus Sancti flagitat, quo conscripta est" (cf. also *In Mich.* 1, 10 PL 25, 1159). It would be rather easy to find similar or even identical affirmations in other ecclesiastical writers of different periods. To quote but only one example, cf. *De imitatione Christi* I,V,2: "Omnis Scriptura sacra Sancto eo Spiritu debet legi, quo facta est." (The author of the latest critical edition of this booklet, Fr. Tiburzio Lupo S.D.B., *De Imitatione Christi libri quattuor*, Libreria editrice Vaticana, 1982, p. 19, refers further to the *Epistola ad fratres de monte Dei*, c. 10, and of course to 2 Pt. 1:21).

18. Cf. what was said above about the historical context of "Divino Afflante." As a matter of fact, there exists here and there a certain unavowed feeling in some ecclesiastical circles that the application of "scientific" exegetical methods to a sacred (inspired) writing can only impair its standing and thereby endanger faith. Cf. in the Ench. Bibl. (nn.522–532) the letter of the Pont. Bibl. Commission, dated 8/20/41, to the archbishops and bishops of Italy, about the self-same subject—a first installment, as it were, of "Divino Afflante."

19. Cf. Hyer Epist. 58 ad Paul 9,1: ". . . dulcius in medulla est. Qui esse vult nucleum, frangit nucem."

20. This poses the question of the *multiplicity* of senses in any writing. This question has been explicitly and thoroughly studied by the medieval theologians in relation to Scripture. St. Thomas should be read in this connection; cf. for instance S.Th. I,1 art. 10 and parallel texts; and, at least for the historical aspect, H. de Lubac, *Exégèse Mediévale. Les quatre sens de l'Ecriture* I,1 (Paris: Aubier, 1959) pp. 110ff., 129ff., etc.

21. I leave here untouched the question of the supreme criterion of the truth of a particular interpretation. I will only say now that, for me, such criterion is in last analysis only internally justifiable in a kind of hermeneutical circle. It goes without saying that other interpretations of the same (sacred) writing, even opposite, can and should always enrich the one which one holds to be true.

22. Cf. vgr. Hermann L. Strack, *Introduction to the Talmud and Midrash* (New York: Atheneum, 1980/6), pp. 93ff., with the reference there; cf. also Frédéric Manns, *La Halakah dans l'Evangile de Mathieu* Antonianum 53 (1978) pp. 4–21, esp. 6ff.

23. Cf. vgr. *Dei Verbum*, n. 12.

24. Cf. Strack, l.c. p. 288, n. 6. The thirteen Middôt would also come from Moses in Sinaï, according to the *Mekhilta on Ex.*21,1 (Rabbi Ishmael).

25. Cf. the beginning of this article and the relevant quotations there from *Dei Verbum*.

26. A parallel drawn already by Origen.

Scripture and Inspiration

Walter Kirchschläger

INTRODUCTION

Any approach to the Bible, be it spiritual or rationalistic, scientific or not, must presume in the reader a basic understanding of it. One advances upon Scripture according to one's attitude toward its pronouncements and the authority one does or does not attribute to it.

Whatever form or method of exegesis is employed, it must first of all define or at least describe the essential features of its object of research. In the case of biblical exegesis, this object is Holy Scripture. The question to be raised therefore is how to find those attributes which are considered indispensable and essential to this book and which must be accepted in order to approach its contents in a correct way, i.e., corresponding to the intention of the author.

This last postulate already indicates the difficulties of the task. Modern exegesis would not deny God's authorship of Scripture of course, but what, then, about the human writers? Many aspects should be listed to indicate the main features of the Bible. One of the most important is certainly the question of divine inspiration. This proposition cannot be merely stated and then set aside. Our task here is to interpret this aspect and to ask: What does it mean that God is the author of the Bible, and what are the implications of this statement?

In addition, it must be noted that the fact of divine inspiration is proclaimed to our contemporary world, that is, to persons educated and influenced by today's ways of thinking which may be described as critical, analytical, historically minded, and open to arguments.

The problem of describing inspiration will be undertaken in several steps. In a first section, the literary aspects of the Bible deserve consideration because

36

we cannot avoid looking at it as a written book. The second part is devoted to a short review of how the Second Vatican Council formulated its approach to Scripture. On that basis, we will then try to outline what inspiration means.

1. SCRIPTURE AS LITERATURE

a. The Historical Setting

This headline may seem provocative but it cannot be denied that Scripture is transmitted to us as a written book. Further, it has never been asserted that Scripture fell from heaven as one complete book. The fact that biblical writings cover a period of more or less one thousand years must not be underestimated. Such a long period of time brought about a continuous development, influencing all areas of human life, such as culture, social environment, and religious thinking. The theological approach toward God and the means employed to express the deeds and words of God are subject to change in history.[1] A comparison of 2 Sam 24:1–4.8–10 and 1 Chron 21:1–9 indicates a change in the attitude toward God and transcendent relations, and this example may stand for many more. Though God's closeness to human beings does not change, the way of reporting and witnessing His deeds does not happen outside of human history but is strictly related to it.

To be more precise: Particular books of the Bible are closely interwoven with the historical situation of their writers and of those first addressed by them, and this relationship extends to the approach to a subject and the means of expression. In order to properly understand the biblical text, exegesis cannot pass over this fact, especially as in our time we are used to thinking in historical categories. The following schematic illustration will help to understand the field of influence.

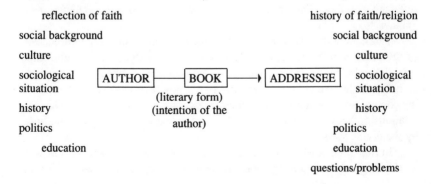

reflection of faith		history of faith/religion
social background		social background
culture		culture
sociological situation	AUTHOR —— BOOK ——▶ ADDRESSEE	sociological situation
	(literary form)	
history	(intention of the author)	history
politics		politics
education		education
		questions/problems

The external appearance of the Bible as a book within one cover is apt to mislead the uninformed reader. Turning a page from the Books of Kings, for instance, to the Books of Chronicles implies a leap of centuries and a fundamental change in the political and cultural situation, not to mention the religious development. To deny the consequences of such chronological progression would imply a refusal to consider the influence on the theological thinking of the Bible's human authors, in this case of the destruction of the First Temple and the exile to Babylon. To be sure, nobody would do that deliberately, but quite often the reader is not even aware of what he is doing by simply turning a page. Such examples could be multiplied and applied as well to the New Testament, though the time intervals may become a little shorter in the latter writings.[2]

The methods of so-called historical-critical exegesis have underlined the above facts, though at times this was admittedly done in a one-sided manner. The method focused on the properties of the text and the literal traces of its manifold origins. Those basic perceptions are valid and no longer under discussion.[3] The problem which emerged and still remains is the question of interpreting those observations in relationship to the divine character of the Bible.

b. Relationships within Scripture

Considering Scripture as literature leads to another observation. If the human origin of the Bible dates back to many different persons writing down several Scriptures in order to inform others or to preserve something for later generations, an intrinsic relationship is established between the human author and those reading or listening to what was put into writing. The written text constitutes the medium of relating the author to his audience, a relationship strongly linked to and determined by the contents of the text. The latter, again, reflects the author's intention to influence the reader in some predetermined manner.[4]

Talking about Scripture, therefore, means at the same time a discussion of the process of written transmission and, particularly, of the relationships established by these writings. We usually consider and define only one aspect, namely, the human author who writes in the power of God. This determines the content of his writings in a manner transcending human abilities. Thus the relationship between the writer and the written text is, at the least, co-defined by the divine spirit.

In this manner of thinking, the link between text and readership as well as the threefold relationship, namely writer–writing–reader, are left open.

Clearly, we must consider Scripture not merely as a book written down once and for all, but as a text in the process of exchange over the centuries. The mere fact that people read the Bible and adapt the human author's thoughts and react to his approach toward God and His deeds implies such a process. In addition, we have to consider the circumstances of inspiration. (cf. part 3).

The consequences are fairly obvious: When we talk about the Bible as a written document, its dynamic character must be considered. Only by the fact that people read this book is an (intellectual) process established. (cf. part 3a).

This dynamic creates a relationship between author and reader. It is influenced by the socio-cultural and historical-religious background of writer as well as reader and, moreover, by content and form of writing.[5] Historical-critical methods will show this in detail.[6]

To avoid misunderstanding, two more observations should be made. What has been said about the reader holds equally true for the listener. There is no doubt that most of the biblical books were written down in order to be publicly read to the assembled people. The main point is that the particular way of writing was an apt and well chosen means of transmission and communication between the writer and those he wanted to address, whether within the immediacy of his own life or throughout later centuries.

At the same time, we must not neglect the fundamentally religious character of biblical writings and their divine background. Stress was placed upon the human implications because that is a decisive part of the Bible which can help to interpret the divine character of Scripture. This will be dealt with in the following section.

2. THE UNDERSTANDING OF SCRIPTURE AT THE SECOND VATICAN COUNCIL

For the first time in the history of Church councils, the Second Vatican Council focused on the Bible in an extraordinary and explicit way. A document dealing especially with the understanding of Scripture was approved.[7] In addition, the Council's other documents are decisively influenced by biblical thinking. Since the theological concepts of the Council are seminal for today's theological thinking,[8] it is fitting to consider its understanding of Scripture more closely.

a. Scripture as a Source of Revelation

The Bible contains the written proclamation of the revelation of God, thus testifying, through the witness in faith of its human authors, to God's loving care of humankind. Though written in human language, Scripture opens our eyes to the greatness of God and manifests His glory. The salvific character of Scripture is closely linked to its content, which reflects the divine decision to save humankind. The Scriptures teach men and women that God is a faithful God, Yahweh and Emmanuel, the God who is favorably disposed toward human beings and in communion with them.

It should be noted in this context that character and form of this divine revelation are in themselves tremendous signs of God's decision toward communion with humankind. The written form produced by human authors is not a hindrance but favorable to the understanding of the Bible by human beings. Yet, there definitely remains a tension between the divine power of these texts and, on the other hand, strong reliance on their human character, which necessarily makes for incompleteness. This aspect of tension is a fundamental characteristic of the Scriptures, and it would be wrong and would cause misunderstanding were we to deny it.

The Council Fathers maintained this aspect of tension. On the one hand, Cardinal Koenig of Vienna, in a famous address to the Council, asked very emphatically that the fact of human historical errors in the Scriptures be faced, and he went on to explicate on several of them.[9] In defining the truth (*veritas*) of the Scriptures, the Council in the main followed his encouragement and, more precisely and more open to future theological discussion than ever before, pronounced the peculiar quality of the Scriptures: "They teach that truth which God, for the sake of our salvation, wished to see confided to the Sacred Scriptures."[10]

On the other hand, the Council furnished a very sound and distinct description of the intrinsic relationship between God as author, and human beings as writers, of the biblical books.

b. Scripture and Tradition

These reflections must be coordinated with other elements of theological thinking and pronouncements of the Church. A consideration of Scripture necessarily implies a reflection on their relationship to the tradition and teaching authority of the Church.

At the very beginning of the Council, it became obvious that this question would be greatly disputed because many different opinions were circulating in the Church. After long discussions prior to the formulation of the *Constitution on Divine Revelation,* Pope John XXIII decided that the relationship between Scripture and Tradition was to be described in a coordinative sense.[11] This allowed space for more research on the subject, without explicitly favoring one of the theological schools or opinions over another. The revelation of God is intended for all human beings throughout the generations, which necessarily implies a process of transmission.[12] The word of God is transmitted from one generation to the next, within the Church and under its authority of guidance and leadership. Thus the Gospel is preserved within the Church as well as in the Bible and in the theological tradition. The latter is still developing through reflection, spiritual experience, and pronouncements by the teaching authority of the Church.[13] Scripture and Church tradition are closely related because of their common origin and their common aim, which lead the Church to rely on revelation, "not from Scripture alone."[14] Scripture, tradition, and the teaching authority of the Church are inseparable; neither one of them can exist without the other two, and all three are related to the spirit of God.[15]

Certain historical priority is admitted in respect to tradition, at least as far as the New Testament is concerned. After the verbal preaching of Jesus and the Apostles, the Kerygma is subsequently pronounced in written form.[16] The Council is well aware of this, yet historical precedent does not cause theological priority. It constitutes, rather, a very close and indispensable link between Scripture and tradition; by stressing this connection, the danger of splitting tradition and Scripture apart is avoided.

One problem remains, of course, despite the careful approach of the Council. It is fairly easy to limit the precise extent of the Bible by definition of a canon—at least in a formalistic way. It is all the more problematic and impossible to the same degree of precision to restrict tradition to certain limits.[17] No doubt exists where that tradition lies within the sphere of dogmatic decisions or where there exists an obvious relationship to the teaching authority of the Church. Yet in addition, tradition contains the living faith attitude within the Church throughout the generations. Whenever it is a question of expressing present day faith, tradition cannot be fully defined in content and limits. Today's theology is not (yet) tradition, though it may eventually assume that status. How many years it has to survive and how long a time of *consensus fidelium* has to precede must be left open.

This problem should not cause theological uneasiness, however. Our inability to set precise limits reflects the intrinsic character of revelation, and this also holds true for Scripture. Both means of revelation must be actualized by the divine spirit, which is not a static, immovable power but a dynamic power. The action of the spirit cannot be fenced in by fixed stakes.

The above observations lead us back again to the main feature of Scripture and its treatment by the Second Vatican Council. The Council's open, yet decisive statements in this regard are obvious. Human features and divine spirit in the Bible's origin are stressed and closely related to the living Church. At the same time, sufficient space is allowed for future reflection on the tension implied in this characterization of Scripture.

3. INSPIRATION AND SCRIPTURE

No doubt must be left about the divine spirit operative in the process of the word of God becoming a written Bible. In the strictly argumentative sense this fact cannot be proved, except by quoting the Bible itself. Yet, the point is not to prove inspiration, but how it can be accepted today, in the light of what was said above.[18]

a. The Dynamic Process of Inspiration

The operating of the divine spirit should not be limited to the writing process of Scripture; nor should it be understood as a mere feature of the Bible proper but, rather, as the dynamic behind these writings.

When we are talking about inspiration we are not confined, therefore, to an analysis of the human author's activity in relation to the divine assistance. Other aspects to be considered are: the relationship between writer and God, between the written book, containing a certain message, and the addressee, and between the addressee and God, as He transmits His word in Scripture.

The Second Vatican Council states unequivocally that revelation contained in the Scriptures is written under the guidance of the spirit of God and that therefore these books have God as their true author. The Council stresses at the same time that, in order to put revelation in writing, God selected human beings, intimating to them what He wanted to be said and doing so according to their abilities and capacities.[19] Scripture contains the true word of God, His revelation, but does so in the words of human beings and is, moreover, linked to history.

It is this dichotomy which may cause difficulties today, and it was this very issue which led the Council to define very carefully the character of truth to be found in the Bible. This truth refers to human salvation and does not necessarily accord with historical or scientific truth. It may, however, transcend the latter, leaving behind historical, scientific, i.e. human, statements, which are merely means to pronounce the truth of God. Thus it is very well possible to recognize some error in Scripture and, at the same time, proclaim Scripture as true and inspired by God. God took into service human beings, not transforming them into super-human creatures. He, then, took into account their limited capacities, and yet He guided them into announcing His truth.

Inspiration thus should be considered as part of the process of writing and must not be confused with dictation. That is the reason why Bible interpretation today is more open toward scientific developments than in the past. Scripture is understood as what it is intended to be by its main Author. God did not want to reveal the unsolved mysteries of His creation, though He might do so in certain instances. What He wanted to announce was His guiding love and His truth, His way of salvation for mankind. These aspects of Scripture must not be confused with one another.

—A book written by a human being is aiming at a certain kind of readership. It is meant to convey a message which is transmitted by its contents and style of writing. Taking into account that in the case of the Bible divine and human authorship combine, a search for the main intent of Scripture must not be confined to human purposes alone, though that is admittedly one of the mistakes sometimes made by modern exegetes. Since God was so personally involved in putting the Bible into writing, its contents are of course properly determined by His intentions. Thus the relationship established between the book and its reader is strongly influenced by the design of God, as contained in Scripture.

—This leads us to the most important point. As the reader receives the Bible not only as one among many other books but as the written pronouncement and revelation of the will of God, he thereby reacts to the fundamental divine intent. In reading the Bible, a person encounters the same divine spirit that stands behind the process of writing down the word of God. This means that inspiration covers not only the process of writing but also the process of receiving, of reading the Bible. God pronounces His word throughout the generations to those who are willing to face it in the Scriptures.

A book is meant to be read, and that holds true also for the Bible. Placed merely on a bookshelf, the divine characteristic of inspiration cannot become effective. Reading a book also requires a certain pre-disposition. Again, this also is true for the Bible. People must know what they are about to do when taking the Bible to hand: they are going to face the word of God. In the process of reading, this word of God is vividly addressed and pronounced to them. It urges them to read or listen, to think and reflect, to assent and to react to the message.

Inspiration, then, may be defined as a dynamic process, directed by the spirit of God. It reflects the initiative of God operative in the human authors of the Bible. Inspiration is aimed at a reader and summons his/her reactions. Each of these aspects is equally important.[20]

b. Further Characteristics of Inspiration

The dynamic understanding of inspiration has certain consequences, and a few of them must be indicated here.

Involving the processes of writing, transmitting, and reading the Bible, inspiration stresses the dialogical character of Scripture. It is very important to realize that reading the Bible is different from reading anything else. This reading implies active listening to the word which is respected as divine; it also implies the disposition to respond to it. The Bible may, of course, be perused differently, but that should not be called "Bible reading."

Some people may object to that as a very subjective approach. Yet, Scripture was never transmitted by a single person but within a faith community witnessing to its perception of the truth. The Bible should be read within such a framework of a community of people believing in God's revelation as testified to in the Scriptures. That is the well founded reason for the Second Vatican Council to stress the interrelationship between Scripture, tradition and teaching authority within the Church. Listening to the word of God also requires comprehension of the individual's place within the community. One cannot interpret the Bible without awareness of the community that one is part of.

—Inspiration constitutes a basic factor of unity within the multiformity of Scripture. It is not necessary to outline the diversity of the single parts of the Bible as far as its specific contents, its time of writing, its literary character and so on are concerned. In their variation, unity is sustained and upheld by the common intent of proclaiming God's faithful and loving inclination toward humankind, which is manifested by the inspiring assistance of God Himself. This characteristic is proper as well as common to all parts of Scripture, distinguishing it from other writings, as well as constituting its uniqueness and importance.

—Perceiving inspiration as a dynamic process assists the reader's ability to understand what he is reading. According to Isaiah 55:10–11, the word of God is powerful: "It shall not return to me void, but shall do my will, achieving the end for which I sent it." The content of Scripture is not confined to those aspects which, once reflected upon, constitute the basis of scriptural exegesis. Propelled by the spirit of God, the Bible contains a "surplus" of meaning, a superfluence of intention and signification, which may or may not be acknowledged by the reader in his spiritual reflection.

This does not supersede scientific exegesis; it rather stresses the fact that scientific interpretation of the Bible should be appreciated as a means of better comprehending Scripture in its spiritual intent. Applying the tools of modern literary science to the Bible is a necessary procedure because of the human part in the origin of the writings. It should be combined with the theological mode of understanding because Scripture contains the word of God, i.e., taking into account the authorship of God. Neglecting either one of these aspects leads to misunderstanding; combining them may possibly bring about an interpretation corresponding to the divine author's intent.

4. CONCLUSION

The concept of inspiration as presented above transcends the limits of time and involves all those who are part of the writing, transmitting, and reading of the Bible. It may serve as model for a more dynamic perception of God's ways with humankind, which are powerful and potent, going beyond the restrictiveness of human life, and constitute a salvific community among men and women that is oriented toward God.

NOTES

1. Cf. W.H. Brownlee, "The Ineffable Name of God," in *Basor* 226 (1977) 39–46; J.L. McKenzie, *Vital Concepts of the Bible* (London, 1967), pp. 31–48.

2. Cf. W. Kirchschlaeger, "Was ist die Bibel?" in *Christlich-Paedagogische Blaetter* 93 (1980) 45–52, esp. 46–47.

3. Cf. the basic consensus in today's introductions to the Bible, e.g.: R. Smend, *Die Entstehung des Alten Testaments* (Stuttgart, 1978); E. Lohse, *Die Entstehung des Neuen Testaments* (Stuttgart, 1972).

4. Cf. L. Griffin, "Hermeneutics," in *The Irish Theological Quarterly* 37 (1970) 235–242, esp. 237–241.

5. Cf. R.F. Collins, "The Matrix of the NT Canon," in *Biblical Theology Bulletin* 7 (1977) 51–59, esp. 54–56.

6. Cf. J. Barr, "Reading the Bible as Literature," in *Bulletin of the John Ryland's Memorial Library* 56 (1973) 10–33.

7. "Dogmatic Constitution on Divine Revelation," *Dei Verbum,* promulgated on November 18, 1965, in A. Flannery, ed., *Documents of Vatican II* (Grand Rapids: Eerdmans, 1975), pp. 750–765.

8. Cf. R.E. Brown, "Rome and the Freedom of Catholic Biblical Studies," in J.M. Myers *et al.,* eds., *Search the Scriptures. New Testament Studies* (Leiden, 1969), 129–150.

9. Cf., for text, W. Kirchschlaeger, *Schriftverstaendnis leicht gemacht* (Klosterneuburg, 1980), pp. 87–89. To this speech also refers J. Beumer, *Die katholische Inspirationslehre zwischen Vatikanum I und II* (Stuttgart, 1966) pp. 93–94.

10. The text reads: ". . . veritas . . . . quam Deus nostrae salutis causa Litteris Sacris consignari voluit . . . " Cf. A. Flannery, *op cit,* p. 756.

11. In his decision of November 14, 1962, Pope John XXIII asked for a new draft of the document by a commission under the co-presidency of Cardinals Ottaviani and Bea. To this refers M. Gilbert, "Le Cardinal Augustin Bea 1881–1968," in *Nouvelle Révue Théologique* 115 (1983) 369–383, esp. 379–380.

12. Cf. *Dei Verbum* II, 7; A. Flannery, *loc. cit,* p. 753.

13. Cf. *Dei Verbum* II, 8; A. Flannery, *loc. cit,* p. 754.

14. The text reads: ". . . non per solam Sacram Scripturam," *Dei Verbum* II, 9; A. Flannery, *loc. cit.*

15. Cf. R. Latourelle, *Theology of Revelation* (New York, 1966), pp. 472–484; Kirchschlaeger, *Schriftverstaendnis,* pp. 84–87.

16. Cf. *Dei Verbum* V, 18–19, Flannery, *loc. cit.,* pp. 760–61. More explicit, Instruction *Sancta Mater Ecclesia,* published by the Pontifical Biblical Commission on April 21, 1964, in AAS 56 (1964) 712–718, esp. 714–716.

17. Cf. Collins, *op. cit.,* pp. 57–58.

18. Basic to this topic is K. Rahner, "Inspiration in the Bible," in *Inquiries* (New York: Herder & Herder, 1964); cf. also Beumer, *op. cit.,* pp. 56–98.

19. The Encyclical Letter *Divino afflante Spiritu,* published by Pope Pius XII on October 20, 1943, in AAS 35 (1943) 297–325, esp. 313–314; *Dei Verbum* III, 11, A. Flannery, *op. cit.,* pp. 356–357; Griffin, *op. cit.,* pp. 235–236; Beumer, *op. cit.,* pp. 83–98.

20. W. Kirchschlaeger, *Schriftverstaendnis,* pp. 59–61.

II. EXEGETICAL TRADITIONS

On the Morality of the Patriarchs in Jewish Polemic and Exegesis*

David Berger

1. THE POLEMICAL WORLD OF THE MIDDLE AGES

On three separate occasions, Naḥmanides denounces Abraham for sinful or questionable behavior.[1] The first of these passages asserts that "our father Abraham inadvertently committed a great sin" by urging Sarah to identify herself as his sister and goes on to maintain that the very decision to go to Egypt was sinful. Later, Naḥmanides expresses perplexity at Abraham's rationalization that Sarah was truly his half-sister; this appears to be an unpersuasive excuse for omitting the crucial information that she was also his wife, and although Naḥmanides proceeds to suggest an explanation, his sense of moral disapproval remains the dominant feature of the discussion. Finally, he regards the treatment of Hagar by both Sarah and Abraham as a sin for which Jews are suffering to this day at the hands of the descendants of Ishmael. The bold, almost indignant tone of these passages is both striking and significant—but it is not typical.

Most medieval Jews were understandably sensitive about ascriptions of sin to the patriarchs, and the situation was rendered even more delicate by the fact that the issue of patriarchal morality often arose in a highly charged context in which Jews were placed on the defensive in the face of a Christian attack. Two thirteenth-century Ashkenazic polemics reflect a somewhat surprising Christian willingness to criticize Jacob as a means of attacking his descendants. Since the patriarch was a Christian as well as a Jewish hero, such attacks on his morality were highly problematical: Jacob may be the father of carnal Israel, but he is the prototype of spiritual Israel as well. While criticisms of

49

this sort are consequently absent from major Christian works, it is perfectly evident that no Jew would have invented them. On the medieval street, then, Christians did not shrink from such attacks on Jews and their forebears. Jacob, they said, was a thief and a trickster; the implication concerning his descendants hardly needed to be spelled out.

In *Sefer Yosef HaMeqanne* we are informed that Joseph Official met a certain Dominican friar on the road to Paris who told him, "Your father Jacob was a thief; there has been no consumer of usury to equal him, for he purchased the birthright, which was worth a thousand coins, for a single plate [of lentils] worth half a coin."[2] The technical impropriety of the reference to usury merely underscores the pointed application of this critique to medieval Jews. The next passage reports a Christian argument that Jacob was a deceiver who cheated Laban by exceeding the terms of their agreement concerning the sheep to which Jacob was entitled, and this criticism is followed by the assertion that Simeon and Levi engaged in unethical behavior when they deviously persuaded the Shechemites to accept circumcision and then proceeded to kill them.[3]

With respect to Jacob, the Jewish response was conditioned by two separate considerations acting in concert. First, religious motivations quite independent of the polemical context prevented the perception of Jacob as a sinner; second, the Christian attack itself called for refutation rather than concession. Hence, Joseph[4] responded with a remarkable suggestion found also in Rashbam's commentary that Jacob paid in full for the birthright; the bread and lentils are to be understood as a meal sealing the transaction or customarily following its consummation. As Judah Rosenthal pointed out in his edition of *Yosef HaMeqanne,* R. Joseph Bekhor Shor reacted with exasperation to the apparent implausibility of this interpretation, which was almost surely motivated by both moral sensitivity and polemical need. As for Laban, the answer to the Christian critique was that Jacob was the real victim of deception, and his treatment of his father-in-law was marked by extraordinary scrupulousness.[5]

Joseph Official goes on to an uncompromising defense of Simeon and Levi which is particularly interesting because this was the one instance in which a concession to the Christian accusation was tactically possible. Jacob, after all, had denounced their behavior, and even if his initial concern dealt with the danger that could result from an adverse Canaanite reaction rather than with the moral issue (Gen. 34:30), his vigorous rebuke of his sons at the end of his life (Gen. 49:5–7) could certainly have supported the assertion that he considered their action morally reprehensible as well as pragmatically unwise. Nevertheless, there is no hint of condemnation in *Yosef HaMeqanne*; if Christians denounced Simeon and Levi, then surely Jews were obliged to defend them, especially since a sense of moral superiority was crucial to the medieval Jewish psyche in general and to the polemicist in particular.[6] Thus, Joseph tells us that the Shechemites regretted their circumcision and were in any event planning to oppress Jacob's family and take over its property; consequently, their execution was eminently justified.[7]

There is a certain irony in the fact that the Christian question in *Yosef HaMeqanne* which immediately follows this series of objections to patriarchal behavior begins, "After all, everyone agrees that Jacob was a thoroughly righteous man; why then was he afraid of descending to hell?"[8] Although this is a return to the Christian stance that we ought to expect, there is in fact one more incident in Jacob's life which Christian polemicists apparently utilized in their debate with Jews, and that is, of course, his deception of his own father.

The anonymous *Nizzahon Vetus* presents the following argument:

> "I am Esau your firstborn" [Gen. 27:19]. One can say that Jacob did not lie. In fact, this can be said without distorting the simple meaning of the verse, but by explaining it as follows: I am Esau your firstborn, for Esau sold him the birthright in a manner as clear as day. It is, indeed, clear that Jacob was careful not to state an outright lie from the fact that when Isaac asked him, "Are you my son Esau?" he responded, "I am" [Gen. 27:24], and not, "I am Esau."
>
> They go on to say that because Jacob obtained the blessings through trickery, they were fulfilled for the Gentiles and not the Jews. The answer is that even the prophet Amos [sic] prayed for Jacob, for he is in possession of the truth, as it is written, "You will grant truth to Jacob and mercy to Abraham, which you have sworn unto our fathers" [Mic. 7:20]. That is, had not the truth been with Jacob, then you would not have sworn to our fathers.[9]

The pattern holds. Once again Christians attack the patriarch's morality, this time the consquences for his descendants are spelled out with explicit clarity, and once again Jewish ingenuity is mobilized for an unflinching, unqualified defense.[10]

Nevertheless, the pattern does not always hold. Polemicists will do what is necessary to win whatever point appears crucial in a particular context, and on one occasion at least we find two Jewish writers displaying very little zeal in defending the questionable action of a biblical hero. Their motivation is hardly mysterious: Jesus had cited this action approvingly.

Jacob ben Reuben and the *Nizzahon Vetus* both comment on the story in Matthew 12 in which Jesus defends the plucking of corn by his hungry disciples on the Sabbath with a reference to David's eating of the shewbread when he was hungry. In his late twelfth-century *Milḥamot HaShem*,[11] Jacob responds as follows:

> How could he cite evidence from David's eating of the shewbread when he was fleeing and in a great hurry? If David behaved unlawfully by violating the commandment on that one occasion when he was forced by the compulsion of hunger and never repeated this behavior again, how could your Messiah utilize this argument to permit the gathering of corn without qualification?

More briefly, the author of the *Nizzahon Vetus* remarks, "If David behaved improperly, this does not give them that right to pluck those ears of corn on the Sabbath."[12] Although Jacob provided mitigation for David's behavior and the *Nizzahon Vetus'* comment might be understood as a counterfactual concession for the sake of argument ("even if I were to agree that David behaved improperly"), the impression of sin is not only allowed to stand but is actually introduced by the Jewish writers. Even more striking, Jacob continued his argument by saying that once Jesus was permitting every act of King David, "why did he not permit sexual relations with married women since David had such relations with the wife of Uriah?" Now, the Talmud had made the most vigorous efforts to deny that Bathsheba was still married to Uriah and, indeed, that David had sinned at all, and the insertion of this question—which was not essential to the argument and is in fact missing from the parallel passage in the *Nizzahon Vetus*—is a telling illustration of the impact of the search for effective polemical rhetoric.[13]

Thus far, we have seen Jewish defenses of biblical heroes for reasons both religious and polemical, and criticisms of their behavior which arose from a sensitive, straightforward reading of the text as well as from polemical concerns. It remains to be noted that the particular ideology of a Jewish commentator, if pursued with sufficient passion, could itself overcome the profound inhibitions against denouncing the morality of the patriarchs. I know of but one example of this phenomenon, but it is quite remarkable.

In his study of Jewish social thought in sixteenth- and seventeenth-century Poland, Haim Hillel Ben Sasson frequently pointed to the animus against the wealthy displayed by the prominent preacher and exegete R. Ephraim Lunshitz. Among many examples of this animus, Ben Sasson draws our attention to Lunshitz's remarks about the rabbinic comment that when Jacob remained alone prior to his wrestling with the angel, his purpose was to collect small vessels that he had left behind. Before Lunshitz, Jews had universally understood this as an exemplification of an admirable trait. Not so the author of the *Kli Yaqar*: "A majority of commentators agree that this angel is Sammael the officer of Esau . . . whose desire is solely to blind (*lesamme*) the eyes . . . of the intelligence." Now, as long as Jacob refrained from the slightest sin, Sammael could not approach him, but once Jacob was guilty of even a small measure of sin, his immunity was lost. And for a rich man like Jacob to remain behind in a dangerous place for a few vessels is indeed the beginning of sin. Jacob had begun to blind himself, "for who is as blind as the lovers of money about whom it is written, 'The eyes of a man are never satiated' (Proverbs 27:20)? . . . Who is such a fool that he would endanger himself for such a small item? Rather, it is a mocking heart which turned him away from the straight path to succumb to such love of money, which causes forgetfulness of God."[14]

What makes this passage all the more noteworthy is that the talmudic source contains an explicitly favorable evaluation: the righteous care so much for their property because they never rob others (*TB Ḥullin* 91a). Moreover, if Lunshitz was uneasy with this talmudic evaluation, nothing was forcing him to mention the passage in the first place; the point is nowhere in the biblical text, and the *Kli Yakar* is in any event a discursive, selective commentary which could easily have skipped the verse entirely. Clearly, he made the point because it served as an outlet for one of his driving passions. Patriarchal immunity from criticism, even in a traditional society, evidently had its limits.

2. BIBLICAL CRITICISM AND JEWISH EXEGESIS IN MODERN TIMES

As the Middle Ages gave way to the modern period, the content and context of this issue were radically and fundamentally altered. Inhibitions against criticizing biblical morality began to crumble, and both Enlightenment ideologues and nineteenth-century scholars gleefully pounced upon biblical passages that appeared morally problematical. In the first instance, the target was the Bible as a whole and, ultimately, Christianity itself; in the second, it was usually the Hebrew Bible in particular, whose allegedly primitive ethics served as a preparation and a foil for the superior morality of the Gospels. In effect, an argument originally directed against Christianity was refocused to attack Judaism alone.[15]

Modern biblical scholarship, then, transformed the essential terms of this discussion, and the transformation was so profound that it ultimately inspired a reaction strikingly different from the standard medieval response. The crucial point is that the attack was no longer on the morality of the biblical personalities. To many Bible critics, the very existence of the patriarchs was in question, and the historicity of specific accounts of their behavior was surely deemed unreliable in the extreme. The attack now was on the morality of the biblical author or authors—an attack that was almost impossible in the premodern period, when the author was ultimately presumed to be God Himself.[16]

Consequently, it now became possible—perhaps even polemically desirable—for traditionally inclined Jews (whether or not they were strict fundamentalists) to take a different approach by driving a wedge between hero and author. There were indeed occasional imperfections in the moral behavior of the patriarchs, but these are condemned by the Torah and required punishment and expiation. Whatever the exegetical merits of this approach, and they are, as we shall see, considerable, it would have been extraordinarily difficult both tactically and psychologically had the attack of the critics still been directed at the patriarchs themselves.

There is, however, a deeper issue here. The assertion that the Bible disapproves of certain behavior was not based on explicit verses of condemnation; rather, it depended on a sensitive reading of long stretches of narrative in which patterns of retribution and expiation emerged. On the simplest level, this approach demonstrated that the morality of the Torah is not inferior to that of Bible critics. On a deeper level, it undercut the effort of some critics to utilize the moral "deficiencies" of certain passages to establish divergent levels of moral sensitivity in the Pentateuch as a whole and in Genesis in particular. But on the profoundest level—at least for some proponents of this approach—it went to the heart of the essential claims of the higher criticism by arguing in a new way for the unity of Genesis. Many of the newly discovered patterns cut through the documents of the critics and emerged only from a unitary perception of the entire book; since the patterns seemed genuine, the only reasonable conclusion was that the unity of Genesis was no less real than its literary subtleties. These observations were not confined to narratives bearing on the morality of the patriarchs, but it is there that some of the most striking examples were to be found.

In the first half of this century, a number of Jewish writers—Martin Buber, Benno Jacob, Umberto Cassutto—began to note such patterns. Before going further, we are immediately confronted by a challenging, almost intractable methodological problem. I have suggested that this revisionist reading of the Bible is rooted in part in traditionalist sentiments, that it presented a new way of responding to people critical of sacred Jewish texts. At the same time, I consider the essential insights justified by an objective examination of the evidence (though my own motives are surely as "suspect" as those of the figures under discussion). Decades ago, Jacob Katz argued that one may not readily assign ulterior motives to someone whose position appears valid in light of the sources that he cites,[17] and more recently Joseph Dan has criticized a work about Gershom Scholem for attributing his view of kabbalah to factors other than his accurate reading of the kabbalistic texts themselves.[18] Fundamentally, these methodological caveats are very much in order, and in certain instances they are decisive. At the same time, undeniable intuitions tell us that even people who are essentially correct can be partially motivated by concerns that go beyond the cited evidence, and there ought to be some way to determine when this is likely to be so. In our case, a figure like Cassutto was clearly concerned not only with the unity of Genesis but with the standing and reputation of the biblical text. Moreover, despite the fact that he was not a fundamentalist and that he was no doubt sincere in his protestation that his essential conclusions flowed solely from an objective examination of the text, the consistency of his conservative tendencies in issue after issue where the evidence could often point either way surely reveals a personality that was inclined to seek traditional solutions.[19]

In contemporary biblical scholarship, such an inclination frequently labels one a neo-fundamentalist whose conclusions are rejected almost *a priori*. This is a manifest error with the most serious consequences. Even people with much stronger traditionalist tendencies than Cassutto can be motivated by those tendencies to seek evidence that turns out to be real. Kepler's laws are no less valid because he sought them as a result of religious convictions. In this instance, a change in the attack on biblical morality liberated and then impelled people with traditionalist inclinations to see things in the text that had gone virtually unnoticed before. At first, these figures were necessarily non-fundamentalists; genuine Jewish fundamentalists would not easily shed their inhibitions about criticizing the patriarchs. With the passage of time, however, even some uncompromisingly orthodox Jews could adopt this approach,[20] while others —probably a majority—would retain unabated the religious inhibitions of the past;[21] "fundamentalism" is far from a monolithic phenomenon.

3. THE BIBLE'S JUDGMENT OF PATRIARCHAL BEHAVIOR: THE CASE OF JACOB'S DECEPTION

Let us turn now to a central example of an approach that we have thus far discussed only in the abstract. At Rebecca's behest, Jacob deceived Isaac by pretending to be Esau and thereby obtained a blessing intended for his brother. We have already seen a medieval Jewish defense of Jacob's behavior, and in the entire corpus of pre-modern Jewish exegesis there is hardly a whisper of criticism.[22] In the twentieth century, however, a number of scholars have noted a series of indications that make it exceedingly difficult to deny that the Torah implicitly but vigorously condemns Jacob's action.

First, the deception was motivated by a misreading of Isaac's intentions. The blind patriarch bestowed three blessings on his children: the first to Jacob masquerading as Esau, the second to Esau, and the third to Jacob. It was only in the third blessing, when he knew for the first time that he was addressing Jacob, that he bestowed "the blessing of Abraham to you and your seed with you so that you may inherit the land in which you dwell which God gave to Abraham" (Gen. 28:4). Though other interpretations of this sequence are possible, the most straightforward reading is that Rebecca and Jacob had gravely underestimated their husband and father. Isaac had indeed intended to bless Esau with temporal supremacy, but the blessing of Abraham—the inheritance of the holy land and the crucial mission of the patriarchs—had been reserved for Jacob from the outset. The deception was pragmatically as well as morally dubious.[23]

Jacob is then subjected to a series of misfortunes and ironies whose relationship to the initial deception cannot be accidental. He must work for his "brother" Laban (Gen. 29:15) instead of having his brothers work for him (Gen. 27:37); he is deceived by the substitution of one sibling for another in the darkness and is pointedly informed that "in our place" the younger is not placed before the older (Gen. 29:26); his sons deceive him with Joseph's garment and the blood of a goat (Gen. 37:31) just as he had deceived his father with Esau's garments and the skin of a goat (Gen. 27:15–16); his relationship with Esau is precisely the opposite of the one that was supposed to have been achieved—Esau is the master (Gen. 32:5,6,19; 33:8,13,14,15) to whom his servant Jacob (32:5,19; 33:5,14) must bow (33:3, and contrast 27:29). Moreover, Jacob's debilitating fear of his brother results from the very act that was supposed to have established his supremacy.[24]

There is, then, ample evidence that Jacob had to undergo a series of punishments to atone for his act of deception. It is almost curious, however, that no one has noted an additional—and climactic—element in this series, which can fundamentally transform our understanding of a crucial aspect of the Joseph narrative. One reason why the point may have been missed is that there are no key words calling it to our attention, and the presence of such words not only alerts the reader but serves as a methodological guide preventing undisciplined speculation. At the same time, we cannot permit ourselves to ignore grand thematic patterns, and in this instance I think that such a pattern has been overlooked.

Leah Frankel, utilizing the "key word" approach, has noted that the root meaning "to deceive" *(rmy)* appears in Genesis three times. The first two instances, in which Isaac tells Esau that his brother deceitfully took his blessing (Gen. 27:35) and Jacob asks Laban why he deceived him (Gen. 29:25), are clearly related to our theme.[25] Perhaps, she suggests, the third instance, in which Simeon and Levi speak deceitfully to Shechem (Gen. 34:13), is intended to indicate that Jacob was "to taste deceit carried out by *sons* [her emphasis]. He would have to stand in the place where his father stood when his son Jacob deceived him."[26] While this approach is not impossible, it seems unlikely; although Jacob suffers indirect consequences from Simeon and Levi's trickery, he is in no sense its object, and the resemblance to his own deception is exceedingly remote.

But there is another act of filial deception in Genesis whose similarity to Jacob's seems unmistakable. Jacob concealed his identity from his father by pretending to be someone else. Similarly, his own misery and anguish reach their climax when his son Joseph conceals his identity and pretends to be something other than what he truly is. The fact that the direct victims of Joseph's deception were the brothers may be the main reason why this observation has been missed, but it is perfectly clear that Jacob is as much a victim as his sons. This point alone should make us reevaluate the key element of the Joseph cycle as the culmination of the process of expiation suffered by the patriarch, and the essential argument does not depend on anything more. But there *is* more. Joseph deceives his father while providing him with food just as Jacob deceived his own father while bringing him the "savory food" which he liked (Gen. 27:7,14,17,25). It is not just that the brothers are Jacob's messengers and will report Joseph's deceptive words to their father (though this is quite sufficient); in the final confrontation between Joseph and Judah, the latter is explicitly a surrogate for Jacob, acting to protect Benjamin *in loco parentis* (Gen. 44:32).[27] Moreover, there is only one other place in Genesis where one person speaks to another with as many protestations of servility as Judah addresses to his "master" in that climactic confrontation; that place, of course, is the description of Jacob's servile behavior toward Esau upon his return from the house of Laban (Gen. 32:4–6, 18–21; 33:1–15).[28] In short, Joseph has not merely concealed his identity from his father; by threatening Jacob's family from a position of mastery, he has actually taken on the role of Esau.[29] The parallel to Jacob's deception is genuinely striking.[30]

4. LITERARY PATTERNS AND THE DOCUMENTARY HYPOTHESIS

During the last decade, J.P. Fokkelman,[31] Robert Alter,[32] and Michael Fishbane[33] have searched the narratives of Genesis for patterns out of purely literary motivations, sometimes with the implicit assumption that the conventional documentary hypothesis remains virtually unchanged no matter how many interlocking themes are discerned. In a reaction to one of Alter's early articles on this subject, I wrote that "I think he underestimates the impact of such literary analysis on the documentary hypothesis. You can allow the 'redactor' just so much freedom of action before he turns into an author using various traditions as 'raw material.' Such an approach must ultimately shake the foundations of the regnant critical theory, not merely tinker with its periphery."[34] More recently, the point has been made with vigor and documentation in David Sykes' dissertation, *Patterns in Genesis*.[35] To Alter's credit, he does confront the question in his later book, and although his conclusions are by no means traditional, they are not wholly consonant with those of critical orthodoxy.[36]

It is becoming clearer from year to year that Genesis is replete with linguistic and thematic patterns of subtlety and power which run through the warp and woof of the entire work. Despite the overwhelming force generated by a critical theory that has held sway for generations, scholars will not be able to hide forever behind the assertion that they are studying the art of a redactor as that word is usually understood. The issue will have to be joined.

NOTES

*It is a pleasure to thank my friend Prof. Sid Z. Leiman for his careful reading of the manuscript. I am particularly grateful to him for the references to *Menahot* and pseudo-Jerome in n. 12, *Sefer Hasidim* and the midrashim in n. 13, and Ehrlich's commentary in n. 21.

1. Commentary to Genesis 12:10, 20:12, and 16:6.

2. *Sefer Yosef HaMeqanne*, ed. by Judah Rosenthal (Jerusalem, 1970), pp. 40–41.

3. *Ibid.*, pp. 41–42.

4. Despite the manuscript, this must refer to Joseph Official and not Joseph Bekhor Shor; cf. the editor's note, and see just below.

5. *Yosef HaMeqanne, loc. cit.*

6. On this point, see my brief discussion in *The Jewish Christian Debate in the High Middle Ages: A Critical Edition of the Nizzahon Vetus with an Introduction, Translation and Commentary* (Philadelphia, 1979), pp. 25–27. I hope to elaborate in a forthcoming study on the problem of exile in medieval polemic.

7. *Ibid.*, p. 42. The persistence of Jewish sensitivity to this story in modern times can perhaps best be illustrated by a contemporary example of Jewish black humor. Simeon and Levi—so the explanation goes—were just as concerned as Jacob about adverse public opinion, and this is precisely why they arranged to have the Shech-

emites undergo the judaizing ceremony of circumcision. Once it would be perceived that it was Jews who had been killed, no one would be concerned.

8. *Ibid.*

9. *The Jewish-Christian Debate*, p. 56.

10. For Rashi's rather different defense of Jacob's veracity as well as the persuasiveness of the version in the *Nizzaḥon Vetus* for later Jews, see my commentary in *The Jewish-Christian Debate*, pp. 246–47. It is worth noting that the *Nizzaḥon Vetus* also reports a Christian argument that Moses' delay in coming down from Mount Sinai (Exod. 32:1) renders him "a sinner and a liar" (p. 67). Mordechai Breuer has suggested (*Sefer Nizzaḥon Yashan*, Jerusalem, 1978, p. 21, n. 57) that this argument *may* have originated among Christian heretics. On the other hand, since it ends with the question "Why did he delay?" it may have been leading to a Christian answer that Moses, who was not really a sinner, was testing the Jews and found them wanting. The ancient rabbis, of course, were generally not faced with the polemical concerns of the Middle Ages, and on rare occasions the Talmud ascribes sin to the patriarchs even where the biblical evidence does not require such a conclusion; see, for example, the accusations against Abraham in TB *Nedarim* 32a.

11. Edited by Judah Rosenthal (Jerusalem, 1963), p. 148.

12. P. 182. It is important to note that the Talmud (TB *Menaḥot* 95b–96a) had suggested a legal justification for what David had done. Note too the anomalous report in pseudo-Jerome cited by L. Ginzberg, *Legends of the Jews* (Philadelphia, 1928), VI, 243.

13. It is, of course, difficult to say what Jacob's view of David's relationship with Bathsheba was in dispassionate, non-polemical moments. For Abravanel's rejection of the rabbinic exculpation of David (TB *Shabbat* 56a), see his commentary to 2 Samuel 11–12. See also the very interesting remarks in *Sefer Ḥasidim*, ed. by J. Wistinetzki (Frankfurt a.M., 1924), no. 46 (p. 43) = R. Margulies' edition (Jerusalem, 1957), no. 174 (p. 181). Cf. also the less striking references in *Midrash Shmuel*, ed. S. Buber (Krakau, 1893), pp. 122–23, and *Seder Eliyyahu Rabbah*, ed. M. Ish-Shalom (Friedmann) (Vienna, 1902), p. 7.

14. *Kli Yaqar* to Genesis 32:35. See Ben Sasson's *Hagut VeHanhagah* (Jerusalem, 1959), pp. 118–19.

15. Cf. the similar medieval phenomenon in which arguments by Christian heretics against the Hebrew Bible were reworked by Orthodox Christians in their polemic with Jews. See *The Jewish-Christian Debate*, p. 6.

16. For an exception, note Luther's remarks on Esther in his *Table Talk:* "I am so hostile to this book that I wish it did not exist, for it judaizes too much, and has too much heathen naughtiness." Cited approvingly by L.B. Paton in his discussion of "the moral teaching of the book" in *The International Critical Commentary: The Book of Esther*, Edinburgh, 1951 (first printing, 1908), p. 96.

17. "Maḥloqet HaSemikhah Bein Rabbi Yaaqov Beirav VehaRalbaḥ," *Zion* 15, sec. 3–4 (1951):41.

18. *Kiryat Sefer* 54 (1979/80): 358–62. Dan does note (p. 361) that even in Scholem's case, extra-textual considerations can play some role.

19. While maintaining that Cassutto's work is essentially anti-traditional, Yehezkel Kaufmann nevertheless pointed to several examples of this conservatism; see "Me'Adam ad Noah," in *Mikivshonah shel HaYezirah HaMiqrait* (Tel Aviv, 1966), p. 217.

20. Yissakhar Jacobson, *Binah BaMiqra*[4] (Tel Aviv, 1960), pp. 33–36; Nehama Leibowitz, *Iyyunim BeSefer Bereshit* (Jerusalem, 1966), pp. 185–88 (English trans., *Studies in Bereshit [Genesis]*, Jerusalem, 1976, pp. 264–69); Leah Frankel, *Peraqim BaMiqra* (Jerusalem, 1981), pp. 102–04, 143–44.

21. Prof. Lawrence Kaplan has called my attention to Rabbi A. Kotler's "How To Teach Torah," *Light* 10, pp. 1ff.; 12, pp. 1f.; 13, pp.1ff.; 15, pp1ff.; 19, pp. 1ff. (1970/71), republished as a pamphlet by Beth Medrash Govoha of Lakewood. A Hebrew version appears in Rabbi Kotler's *Osef Hiddushei Torah* (Jerusalem, 1983), pp. 402–11. "If there were any fault," writes the author,"—however slight (Hebrew: *daq min hadaq*)—in any of the Ovos [patriarchs], the very essence of the Jewish people would have been different" (English pamphlet, p. 6 = Hebrew, p. 404). Rabbi Kotler makes it clear that his work is a reaction to modern heresy *(kefirah)*, which perceives the patriarchal narratives as ordinary stories. On the other hand, Prof. Kaplan notes that the popular *Pentateuch and Haftorahs* edited by Rabbi J.H. Hertz (1936) extols Scripture precisely because it "impartially relates both the failings and the virtues of its heroes" (commentary to Gen. 20:12, citing one of the passages from Nahmanides with which we began). Similarly, Arnold B. Ehrlich asserts that Scripture does not conceal the faults of the patriarchs; see *MiKra Ki-Pheschuto*, New York, 1898 (reprinted, New York, 1969), I, pp. 33, 73 (to Gen. 12:14, 16 and 25:27); his German *Randglossen zur Hebräischen Bibel*, Leipzig, 1908 (reprinted, Hildesheim, 1968) omits the first and more important passage. Ehrlich, a brilliant maverick who was neither a traditionalist nor a conventional critic, was in many respects *sui generis* and resists inclusion in any neat classificatory scheme. Finally, Rabbi Shalom Carmy has called my attention to the willingness of representatives of the nineteenth-century Musar movement to acknowledge minor imperfections in the patriarchs as part of the movement's special approach to the analysis of human failings.

22. David Sykes, in his dissertation, *Patterns in Genesis*, Bernard Revel Graduate School (Yeshiva University, 1984), notes *Zohar, Vayeshev*, 185b, which indicates that Jacob was punished for this act because even though something is done properly, God judges the pious for even a hairbreadth's deviation from the ideal. He also points to the Yemenite manuscript cited in *Torah Shelemah* vol. 6, p. 1432, #181 (where the editor also notes the *Zohar* passage), which indicates that Jacob was deceived by his sons with a goat (Gen. 37:31) just as he had deceived his own father with a goat (Gen. 27:16). See also below, note 24.

23. *Binah BaMiqra, loc. cit.* Cf. also Malbim on Gen. 27:1 and Leibowitz, *Iyyunim*, pp. 193–95.

24. For pre-modern references to such arguments, see note 22; *Midrash Tanhuma*, ed. S. Buber (Vilna, 1885), *Vayeze* 11, p. 152, and the parallel passage in *Aggadat Bereshit*, ed. by S. Buber (Krakau, 1902), ch. (48)[49], p. 99, where Leah tells

Jacob that he has no right to complain about being deceived since he too is a deceiver (though the midrash does not explicitly endorse her criticism); Eliezer Ashkenazi (sixteenth century) *Ma'asei HaShem* (Jerusalem, 1972), vol. 1, p. 115b, who comments on Laban's remark about the younger and older but apparently considers it evidence of Laban's nastiness rather than Jacob's culpability. Note too *Genesis Rabbah* 67:4, which speaks of later Jews crying out in anguish because of Esau's agonized exclamation in Gen. 27:34, and the somewhat more ambiguous midrash of unknown provenance cited by Rashi on Psalms 80:6, in which Jews shed tears as a result of Esau's tears; see Leibowitz, *Iyyunim*, p. 190. Such isolated observations over a period of more than a millennium and a half do not, I think, undermine or even significantly affect the thesis of this paper. For twentieth-century references, often containing additional arguments, see Martin Buber, *Die Schrift und ihre Verdeutschung* (Berlin, 1936), pp. 224–26; Benno Jacob, *Das Erste Buch der Tora: Genesis* (Berlin, 1934), p. 591 (abridged English translation, New York, 1974), pp. 197–98; Umberto Cassutto, *La Questione della Genesi* (Florence, 1934), esp. p. 227; *idem, Torat HaTe'udot* (Jerusalem, 1959), pp. 55–56 = *The Documentary Hypothesis* (Jerusalem, 1961), pp. 63–64; *idem,* "Ya'aqov," *Enẓiqlopediyyah Miqrait (EBH)*, vol. 3, cc. 716–22; Jacobson, Leibowitz, and Frankel (see note 20); Nahum M. Sarna, *Understanding Genesis*, (New York, 1966), pp. 183–84; Jacob Milgrom in *Conservative Judaism* 20 (1966):73–79; J.P. Fokkelman, *Narrative Art in Genesis* (Assen and Amsterdam, 1975), pp. 128–30, 200, 223, 227; Sykes, *op. cit.* (note 22). With the exception of Fokkelman, all these figures, whether they are fundamentalists or not, more or less fit the traditionalist typology that I have proposed. Needless to say, the evident validity of many of these exegetical suggestions must (or at least should) eventually affect biblical scholars of all varieties.

25. Cf. *Tanḥuma* and *Aggadat Bereshit* in the previous note.

26. *Peraqim BaMiqra*, p. 104.

27. It may be worth asking (with considerable diffidence) whether Judah's status as a surrogate for Jacob may help us resolve an old, intractable crux. In Joseph's second dream, the sun, moon and eleven stars, presumably symbolizing his father, mother, and brothers, bow down to him (Gen. 37:9–10). But his mother was already dead at the time of the dream; less seriously, Jacob does not bow to Joseph until Genesis 47:30, by which time our intuition tells us (I think) that the dreams ought to have already been fulfilled. *Perhaps* two of the brothers who bow to Joseph represent both themselves and a parent; Judah is the surrogate for Jacob, and Benjamin, who is pointedly described as his mother's only surviving child (Gen. 44:20), is the representative of Rachel. Joseph's parents bow down to him through their offspring.

28. For whatever this is worth, Jacob addresses Esau as "my master" seven times in these verses (32:6, 19; 33:8, 13, 14 [twice], 15 [32:5 is not addressed to Esau]) and Judah addresses Joseph as "my master" seven times in his final speech (44:18 [twice], 19, 20, 22, 24, 33). Since seven is clearly a significant number and since Jacob is explicitly said to have bowed to Esau seven times (Gen. 33:3 ["complete subjection," says Fokkelman, p. 223]), it is at least possible that this is more than coincidence.

29. Note too that Jacob was most concerned with Esau's threat to Rachel and her

child (Gen. 33:2), and it was Rachel's child Benjamin who was singled out for persecution by the Egyptian viceroy. Finally, Prof. David Shatz has called my attention to the use of the rare verb *stm* (to hate) with regard to both Esau's hatred of Jacob (Gen. 27:41) and the brothers' fear that Joseph would hate them (Gen. 50:15).

30. The fact that Joseph's actions were no doubt motivated by other factors involving his brothers does not, of course, refute the perception that we are witnessing the final step in a divine plan to purge Jacob of his sin. It is, in fact, possible that an even later incident in Genesis is related to Jacob's deception of Isaac. The successful expiation of that sin may be symbolized by Jacob's ability, despite his failing eyesight, to discern the difference in the destinies of his older and younger grandsons (Gen. 48:10–20). Cf. Benno Jacob, *Das Erste Buch,* p. 884 (called to my attention by David Sykes), and Cassutto, *La Questione della Genesi,* p. 232. (It need hardly be said that this new approach does not end with a denunciation of biblical heroes. After a process of retribution and moral development, the ethical standing of the patriarch is beyond reproach.) Finally, it must be stressed that other moral questions like the scriptural evaluation of the treatment of Hagar and the behavior of the young Joseph are also susceptible to this mode of analysis.

31. See n. 24.

32. *The Art of Biblical Narrative* (New York, 1981).

33. *Text and Texture* (New York, 1979).

34. *Commentary* 61:3 (March, 1976), 16. It may be worth asking whether Shakespeare has ever been described as the redactor of the various Hamlet documents.

35. See n. 22. My affirmation of the validity of this general approach does not, of course, imply an endorsement of every pattern or set of patterns that has been suggested, and it is self-evident that some proposals will be more persuasive than others. This mode of interpretation will always be vulnerable to the charge of arbitrary and subjective eisegesis. Nevertheless, such is the fate of almost all literary analysis, and a combination of methodological guidelines and a healthy dose of common sense can minimize, though never eliminate, undisciplined speculation. In any case, I am thoroughly persuaded that the recent literature contains more than enough convincing examples to sustain the essential point.

36. P. 20 and esp. ch. 7 (pp. 131–154). In the present climate, it requires some courage to express such views, and Alter has already been accused of involvement in *(horribile dictu)* "the new fundamentalism" (and he has already denied it); see *Commentary* 77:2 (February 1984):14. Cf. also Fokkelman's very brief comment on the issue in *Narrative Art,* p. 4.

Reflections on Catholic Exegesis and Jewish-Christian Dialogue at the Pontifical Biblical Institute

Maurice Gilbert, S.J.

The following considerations reflect the work accomplished and methods developed by the Pontifical Biblical Institute (PBI) in Rome. This Jesuit institution prepares theologians for their future work all over the world. It is one of the foremost Catholic post-graduate schools of theological training and has made noteworthy contributions to the Jewish-Christian dialogue. A discussion of the PBI's work will add still another dimension to the body of knowledge available to participants in the dialogue between Christians and Jews.

By examining the importance of the PBI in this manner, I will be able to illustrate the change in Roman Catholic biblical awareness since Vatican II and its implications for the Jewish-Christian dialogue. To do so, I am suggesting three approaches to this subject. The first will present a number of facts to show what has been done in Catholic exegesis thus far to promote a better understanding of Jewish tradition and also what has been done to promote scholarly cooperation. The second part will describe the basic methodological principles which are operative in Catholic exegesis today. The third and shortest part raises some exegetical questions on which dialogue between Jewish and Christian specialists could shed light.

I. THE WORK OF THE PONTIFICAL BIBLICAL INSTITUTE

Cecil Roth, in the *Encyclopedia Judaica* (X, 8–9), wrote: "In the face of considerable opposition from his colleagues, [Ignatius of] Loyola himself insisted on disregarding the racial principle." Sad to say, his attitude on this point was set aside less than forty years after his death.

In the famous *Ratio Studiorum* of the Society of Jesus published during the generalate of Father Claude Aquaviva, in 1599, after fifty years of preparation, we read the following rules, numbered 9, 10 and 11, which concern the professor of Scripture:

> 9. Should there be in the writings of Hebrew Rabbis any useful information to be quoted in favor of the Latin Vulgate or on Catholic dogmas, they should quote them in such a way that they are not given a place of authority, or in such a way to arouse interest in them, especially if they are among those who wrote after the time of Christ our Lord.

> 10. In researching other aspects of Rabbinic writings, even in trying to demonstrate their errors, let them not take too much trouble. The same applies to the reading of some Christian interpreters who followed the Rabbis too closely.

> 11. Above all, let them not give extreme importance to the vowel points invented by Rabbis. Let them weigh carefully our Latin texts, the Septuagint, or other early interpreters who read when vowel points did not exist.

I have insisted on quoting these texts because there is no doubt that they had a great influence at least on Jesuit exegetes who are numerous and important from the end of the sixteenth century up to the first half of the seventeenth century. From this time to the end of the nineteenth century, Catholic exegesis was stagnant, and even declined.

The beginning of the twentieth century is clearly a period of renewal. A few well-known Catholic exegetes show knowledge of Jewish tradition and one can list important studies on the subject. First of all, let me mention the work of Fr. Lagrange, O.P., founder of the Ecole Biblique de Jérusalem, *Le Messianisme chez les Juifs* (Paris, 1909). Although this book needs to be brought up to date as regards its sources and because of the mentality with which the author approaches Jewish documents—solely for light it can shed on Christian Messianism—we can still recognize in this work a valuable contribution. It is still quoted and is probably the first work that a Catholic scholar of this century has devoted to ancient Jewish tradition.

The following year, 1910, two doctoral theses in Bible studies were presented to the Pontifical Biblical Commission. The first was by Jean-Baptiste Frey, of the Society of Saint Sulpice, *La Théologie juive au temps de Jésus*

Christ, comparée à théologie néo-testamentaire. The thesis was highly praised but was not published. Later on the author published important studies on the religious thought of ancient Judaism in *Revue biblique* and *Biblica.* More significantly, he published the two volumes of the *Corpus Inscriptionum Judaicarum* that he had completed before he died, in 1936. This work had the honor of being republished in 1975 by KTAV (New York). From 1925 on J.B. Frey had been secretary of the Pontifical Biblical Commission.

The other thesis presented to the Biblical Commission in 1910 was the work of J. Bonsirven, a priest from the diocese of Albi (France). The title was, "Eschatologie rabbinique d'après les Targums, Talmuds, Midraschs. Ses éléments communs avec le Nouveau Testament." But this thesis was not accepted for reasons which are not known. The correspondence between the author and his bishop (published by Marcel Becamel, in *Bulletin de littérature ecclésiastique, 71 [1970], pp. 262ff.)* does not give a conclusive answer. It seems that it was not the topic that displeased the Commission but rather the author himself, whose orthodoxy was wrongly suspect. This was at the height of the Modernist crisis. Later J. Bonsirven entered the Society of Jesus and published two volumes on *Le Judaïsme palestinien au temps de Jésus Christ* (Paris, 1934–35), of which his thesis comprises a part of the first volume. He continued his research in the area in which he had specialized and published, among others in 1955, a well-known collection, *Textes rabbiniques des deux premiers siècles chrétiens pour servir à l'intelligence du Nouveau Testament.* It is a useful anthology though it needs to be redone following exactly the original texts that Bonsirven often only summarizes. At the time, J. Bonsirven was professor at the Pontifical Biblical Institute, a post he had held since 1948.

It is clear, therefore, that from the beginning of the century, long before the Second Vatican Council, Catholic exegetes, some of whom were foremost in the field, had already paved the way for the study of Judaic sources.

In the new *Ratio Studiorum* of the Jesuits, published in 1941 by the General Father Ledokowsky, the texts on the study of Jewish tradition that I quoted earlier, and that were still found in the 1832 edition of *Ratio Studiorum* prepared by Father Roothaan, were no longer present. Even before 1941, a change significant for its time had taken place at the Pontifical Biblical Institute, under the leadership of Augustine Bea who became Rector in 1930. Following the directives of the Apostolic Constitution on ecclesiastical studies "Deus scientiarum Dominus" issued in 1931, the Biblical Institute drew up new statutes, approved in 1934. Article 43 directs that, among the special areas of study newly created, the curriculum of the Institute is to include courses in the history of Mishnaic and Talmudic literature, and courses in the post-biblical Hebrew and Aramaic languages (Mishnaic, Targumic and Talmudic).

I mention this fact not only to highlight aspects of the policy of Fr. Bea's administration, but especially because the Biblical Institute became at this time one of the centers where the majority of future Catholic exegetes were trained: in 1934 the Institute had ninety-two students from all over the Western world.

From 1934 on, an introduction to the great Judaic tradition was offered regularly to the students at the Institute. Limiting myself to the years preceding Vatican II, I list the following main courses:

—L. Semkowsky offered every second year, from 1934 to 1943, an introduction to Mishnaic Hebrew, through the reading of the tractate *Berakot*.

—U. Holtzmeister offered also every second year, from 1935–1946, an introduction to the Talmuds.

—M. Zerwick offered four times, between 1936 and 1952, a history of Judeo-Hellenistic literature.

—A. Vaccari offered a course, in 1937 and in 1952, on the Targums.

—E. Zolli, from 1945–1956, offered every year, a course on a tractate of the Mishnah and another on texts of the Targum.

—J. Bonsirven offered three times between 1949–1955 a course or a seminar on the theology of ancient Judaism.

—P. Boccaccio offered every year from 1953–1965 a seminar on some texts of Qumran.

All of this shows that we were not starting from zero at the time of the Council. But the Council urged us to greater openness. As is stated in n. 4 of *Nostra aetate*, ''Since the spiritual patrimony common to Christians and Jews is thus so great, this sacred Synod wishes to foster and recommend that mutual understanding and respect which is the fruit above all of biblical and theological studies and of brotherly dialogue.'' During the preliminary deliberations, Msgr. Elchinger, Bishop of Strasbourg, said, ''Studies on the Law or the Prophets (or even on what we refer to as the 'Writings'), pursued by Jews and Christians with sufficient background and working together, would surely yield great spiritual benefits.''

In 1966, commenting on the section of the Council's document quoted above, Cardinal Bea wrote that the dialogue desired at the biblical and theological levels would benefit both parties, and that therefore Catholics too would progress in their knowledge of revealed truth through these efforts. He added that even though *Nostra aetate* did not mention collaboration explicitly, it is still one of the general means recommended by the declaration (Cf. A. Bea, *The Church and the Jewish People,* London 1966, pp. 131–132).

In the ''Guidelines and suggestions for the application of the declaration

'Nostra aetate' '' signed in 1974 by Cardinal Willebrands, the same ideas are made more explicit. We read, ''Competent people will be encouraged to meet and study together the main problems deriving from the fundamental convictions of Judaism and of Christianity.'' And especially, ''Research into problems bearing on Judaism and Jewish-Christian relations will be encouraged among specialists, particularly in the fields of exegesis, theology, history and sociology. Higher institutions of Catholic research, if possible in association with other similar Christian institutions and experts, are called upon to contribute to the solution of such problems. Wherever possible, chairs of Jewish studies will be created and collaboration with Jewish scholars encouraged.''

What has been done to meet the Council's expectations, since the close of Vatican II in 1965, at the Pontifical Biblical Institute?

The Institute's publications seldom concerned Judaism before the Council, except for J. Bonsirven's *Textes rabbiniques,* but now a number of important works have been published. I can count at least ten. Some of these studies are by Catholics. For example Prof. R. Le Déaut published a study on the Passover and the Targum of Chronicles; Prof. J. Fitzmyer, the *Genesis Apocryphon* of Qumran and an anthology of Aramaic texts. There are also works by Jewish scholars: The *Massorah Gedolah,* edited by Prof. G. Weil; the Aramaic version of Ruth, edited with commentary by Prof. E. Levine; the fragments of the Targums of the Pentateuch, edited and translated by Prof. M. Klein. In addition, every year Jewish scholars publish articles in our periodical *Biblica.* For example, some of the authors who have published in the issues of the past few years: Prof. A. Malamat, Z. Ben Hayyim, S. E. Loewenstamm, E. Levine, M. Ohana, G. Vajda, M.H. Goshen-Gottstein, M. Klein, M. Weinfeld, M. Heltzer, Y.T. Radday, S. Talmon, E. Tov, H. Jason, H. Tadmor, M. Cogan, H.N. Rosel, M. Zipor, Z. Ben-Barak and M.I. Gruber. Since the Council, then, scholarly publications have also become a meeting-ground for successful collaboration. And I would like to add that this is real collaboration where an author and the editors of a journal, working together in quest of truth, seek and reach a common accord.

Another aspect of cooperation is the training of future Catholic exegetes. For the past ten years a rather original and most effective method has been used. The Biblical Institute sends about twenty students a year to the Hebrew University in Jerusalem. For seven months (a summer semester and a fall semester), these students follow courses in the Hebrew language, in archeology, geography and history given by professors of the Hebrew University, and this program becomes part of the student's curriculum toward the licentiate in biblical studies awarded by the Institute. We are proud of this collaboration which provides approximately one-fourth of our students with a relatively long period of meaningful contact with the Jewish world.

Finally, without listing the courses given at the Institute by professors who are specialists in Judaism and who follow a tradition dating back some fifty years now, it should be noted that in most of the doctoral theses presented today at the Biblical Institute, particularly those concerning the New Testament, there is often a section studying the chosen topic in the light of ancient Jewish sources. This too is a consequence of the renewed spirit that emerged from the Council.

II. PRINCIPLES OF EXEGESIS

First of all it is necessary to place exegesis in its Catholic context. Leaving aside for a moment what Vatican II formally stated, I will quote from the statutes of the Pontifical Biblical Institute because they express the ideals of the exegetical work done there, and while remaining faithful to the Catholic tradition they also insist on a high scholarly standard in research as in teaching and in publications.

Without being substantially different from the principles enunciated in the 1934 statutes of the Biblical Institute, the new statutes do spell out the Institute's policy in clear agreement with Vatican II. These statutes date back to 1969, and so far we have not judged it useful or opportune to modify them except on one point.

The chapter on which I would like to comment is entitled: "General Methods of Teaching." The first part reads: "Because God chose to speak through men in a human way, Holy Scripture, by the very fact that it is also the work of men, must be analyzed and taught with methods that are normally used in the study of ancient literatures, without neglecting any help that secular scholarship can provide toward better understanding."

It goes on to state: "Because Holy Scripture is the Word of God, it must also be read and interpreted in the light of the same Spirit with which it was written; the study of Scripture then must take into account the content and the unity of all Scripture, the living Tradition of the whole Church, and the Analogy of Faith."

These two complementary texts result explicitly—the notes are clear on this—from n. 12 of the Constitution *Dei Verbum* of Vatican II, whose main argument they summarize. These texts depend essentially on the Council's statement on inspiration which immediately precedes it (n. 11): the author of Holy Scripture is both God himself and the sacred authors that He chose. Because these men (still from *Dei Verbum*, n. 11) are true authors, or (from *Dei*

Verbum, n. 12) "because God spoke through men, in a human way," Scripture, which is also their work, must be studied and taught using all the available means of scholarship, including secular ones, that allow us to perceive better still what the sacred authors really meant to say *(Dei Verbum, n. 12).* The Council insisted on the necessity of studying literary genres and drew its inspiration from the encyclical of Pius XII "Divino afflante Spiritu," which appeared in 1943. The Council was thus making its own the teachings of Pius XII. It is perhaps helpful to recall that at the opening of the Council, literature which criticized historico-critical exegesis had been distributed. In a private document entitled "The Historicity of the Gospels," which was made available to the bishops at the Council, Cardinal Bea showed that the methods of literary genres specifically on the question of history could be applied to the synoptic Gospels, without accepting Bultmann's extreme position. In its statements about literary genres in Scriptures, without distinguishing Old Testament or New Testament, the Council indirectly followed not only Pius XII but also Cardinal Bea. The study of literary genres requires comparisons with non-biblical as well as biblical texts using "the methods that are usually used in the study of ancient literature," as we find it expressed in the text of the statutes of the Biblical Institute quoted above.

The next article from the same statutes lists some of "the methods, usually used," whereas the Council, for reasons peculiar to the time in which it was held, limited itself to literary genres only, without excluding other methods. "It is therefore necessary to acquire a direct knowledge of biblical texts in their original language. This comes first and foremost. It is also necessary to know the state of the questions being asked, to acquire a true scholarly method of study, to know the meaning and the teaching of Scripture. All of these areas make up the content of the courses given. But it is also necessary "to acquire a sufficient knowledge of the culture, the religion and the history of the Ancient Near East, of the Jewish and of the Hellenistic world, insofar as this leads to a better understanding of Scripture."

This text is of major importance. The knowledge of the Jewish world is linked to that of the Ancient Near East in general and also to that of the Hellenistic world. In this way all of Scripture, Old Testament and New, is linked to the context that gave it birth during the different historical periods. Furthermore we are told that adequate knowledge of the context is necessary "insofar as this leads to a better understanding of Scripture."

In a later article describing the course of studies, the statutes include the following among the subsidiary subjects: literature from the Judeo-Hellenistic world, from Qumran, the Targum, the Mishna, Talmud and Midrash, as well as the Hebrew and Aramaic languages as found in post-biblical texts.

Other subsidiary disciplines help to understand better those civilizations that were contemporaneous with Scripture, or which transmitted it to us.

The study of ancient Judaism is thus not the only one necessary for Catholic exegetes. This study is done essentially in view of Scripture and to shed light on it. The purpose is precise and in a way restrictive. What I mean is that not all questions concerning Judaism are to become an object of study for the exegete, for example, the great movements of the Kabbala or of Hassidism, or even the complex and terrible sufferings experienced by Jews during this century. But remaining in the sphere of biblical exegesis, I think we in fact reach the core of the questions and problems, because the Hebrew Bible is at the heart of the life and existence of Judaism as is the Old and New Testament for Christianity.

But it seems to me that today's Catholic is considering the texts of Jewish tradition in a new way. He does not read these texts only to draw from them what he considers helpful in understanding the New Testament, as J. Bonsirven would have done for his anthology of Rabbinical texts. Rather, he tries to understand these texts and the tradition from within and for its own sake, so as to avoid tendentiously reading into the text meanings which it will not bear. In this way he will study Jewish tradition with greater respect and candor.

The second text from the statutes of the Biblical Institute quoted above, goes on to say that being inspired, that is, having God as author, Scripture is the Word of God. It must be read and interpreted not only with the scholarly methods referred to above, but "with the same Holy Spirit by whom it was written." This phrase comes originally from Saint Jerome (PL 26, 417A) who refers directly to the necessity of seeking from the Spirit of God the help that the exegete needs in fulfilling his role well.

I believe it is important for the exegete to be in touch with his faith at the deepest level. The Bible is not for him just another book to be studied as one studies Shakespeare or Virgil or Homer. The Bible is for the believer at the center of his life. As Paul VI said to Italian Catholic exegetes on September 25, 1970, one must "look for a certain similarity of interest with the problem and the subject dealt with in the text so as to dispose himself to listen to it with an open mind." We probably find here the reason why, since the Council and because of it, the "Lectio Divina" has become so meaningful to many in the Catholic world, especially among the young; it is a return to the patristic and medieval tradition of the Church. I also believe that many Catholic exegetes are gradually having this experience. And I wonder whether a prayerful reading of the Bible, of the Psalms especially, should not be done more often by the Catholic and Jewish exegetes together.

A. The Unity of Scripture

It follows from the Council (and our statutes simply reflect its teaching) that the exegete must keep in mind the content and the unity of Scripture if he wishes to discover the real meaning of the biblical text. This affirmation is easy to understand, as we believe that all of Scripture has God as its author, yet it is probably the first time that a document of the Church's Magisterium states it quite so clearly. Therefore the Catholic exegete must ever keep in mind the unity of Scripture.

There is at the outset a very real problem: Christians and Jews do not have the same canon of the Bible. The Council certainly refers to the unity of the two Testaments, Old and New. On this fundamental issue Catholic exegetes differ from Jewish exegetes. On the other hand this also means that the Catholic exegete must avoid the Marcionite temptation to reject the Hebrew Bible, the Old Testament, as if the Saving Lord were not its author. Pius XI warned against this in his encyclical against National Socialism, "Mit brennender Sorge," in 1937.

The Catholic point of view does not see any conflict between the two Testaments, but rather seeks to find the link or the passage that leads from one to the other, from the Old to the New, a passage implying both a certain difference but not contradiction, and a certain continuity. For example, Catholic exegetes nowadays know very well that we must not consider the God of the Hebrew Bible as the God of wrath as if He had revealed His mercy only in the New Testament. To illustrate this the expression of the law of the Talion (retaliation) in the Hebrew Bible and the discourse of Jesus on the Mount must be studied with greater attention than has often been done in the past. I have tried to do this in an article which appeared in January 1984 in *Christus*, a periodical published in Paris. Neither do contemporary exegetes say that the Covenant with Abraham and the one which was later established on Sinai with the whole chosen people are now obsolete. The Catholic position is not satisfied with this simplistic caricature of truth. As Paul says, "God never takes back his gifts or revokes his choice" (Romans 11:29; cf. *Documentation Catholique*, 64 (1982) 830–836).

The difficulty in studying the connection between Old Testament and New is made more complicated because Christians themselves do not agree on the content of the Old Testament. Catholics, as we know, accept as part of the Old Testament not only the Hebrew Bible but also certain books that have come down to us in Greek, including Ben Sirach of which we have today two-thirds of the Hebrew text. Now these last mentioned books, which are considered the inspired work of God by Catholics, help us to understand better this transition to the New Testament. On the other hand, these books are also the fruit of Judaism and can often be understood correctly only in the light of other texts belonging to the Jewish tradition. The same is true as regards the relationship between Torah and Wisdom, which are so important in Judaism: Torah is Wisdom.

Awareness of the unity between the two Testaments has also resulted in the recent great strides made in what is called Biblical Theology. We can certainly admit that before Pius XII's "Divino afflante Spiritu" in 1943, Catholic exegesis lived in a certain fear and did not dare broach the teaching of the more theological aspects of Scripture, ever since the Modernist crisis at the beginning of the century. On this point Pius XII's encyclical was a liberating document, but it also meant that Catholic exegetes bore a heavy responsibility for the future. Since 1943, and more clearly still from Vatican II on, the study of biblical theology has developed in the world of Catholic exegesis. In a certain way, I would say that Catholic exegesis was transformed.

To become aware of this it is enough to compare the publications of the Biblical Institute before 1943 with those that followed. Before 1943, studies were made in philology, history, archeology, but later the topics dealt much more frequently with the theological content of Scripture. This change is also found if we compare the *Dictionnaire de la Bible* de F. Vigouroux (Paris 1895–1912) with its *Supplément au Dictionnaire de la Bible* which was started in 1928, and by 1949 had reached the letter H and is still coming out. The later volumes contain many more articles on biblical theology. Another example is the famous *Vocabulaire de théologie biblique,* compiled by X. Léon-Dufour in the early 1960's, with the collaboration of some seventy French-speaking exegetes. This work has now been translated into many languages. All these works, based on a serious historico-critical analysis of the literal meaning of the biblical text, show the development of many theological themes throughout the whole of Scripture.

B. *The Living Tradition*

The same statutes of the Biblical Institute add that the exegete must keep in mind the living Tradition of the whole Church with the attention given to the content and the unity of Scripture as a whole. From the Catholic point of view, this attention can only be brought about in harmony with Tradition and, as the Council also says, with the analogy of faith, about which I will speak later.

What is meant by the living Tradition of the whole Church? The Second Vatican Council explained the term, at the end of a long and hard debate, in *Dei Verbum* (n. 8). The Church firmly believes that God revealed Himself in the Old Testament and in a unique way in Jesus whom Catholics recognize as Messiah and God's only Son, and that this God continued to speak through the Apostles whom Jesus sent out to preach the Gospel that He had brought. Through their preaching, their example, the structure that they gave to the Church, as well as by their writings preserved in the New Testament, the Apostles accomplished their mission with the help of the Holy Spirit and transmitted it to their successors down to today and for all ages to come.

Throughout the ages therefore, God continues to speak to the Church. Paul's word of warning was, ". . . keep the traditions that we taught you, whether by word of mouth or by letter" (2 Thes. 2:15). This faithful transmission of the deposit of Faith given to the Apostles is what we mean by Tradition. But it lives on because, under the guidance of the Holy Spirit, it continues to grow in the Church all through the centuries, in the sense that union with God and with Jesus, contemplation and study, interior spiritual understanding received from the Spirit and the teaching of the successors to the Apostles, all these open the minds of Christians to understanding the realities brought by Tradition, the revealed Truth. The Fathers of the Church, who, for the first eight centuries of Christian history, enlightened Christians by their writings, witness to the life-giving presence of this Tradition. Scripture is the Word of God entrusted by Jesus and by the Holy Spirit to the Apostles; it is Tradition that passes it on to their successors to build up the Church.

"Sacred Tradition and Sacred Scripture," says *Dei Verbum* (n. 10), "form one sacred deposit of the word of God, which is committed to the Church." The whole People of God lives from this one deposit of faith. But "the task of authentically interpreting the word of God . . . has been entrusted exclusively to the living teaching office of the Church, whose authority is exercised in the name of Jesus Christ. This teaching office is not above the word of God, but serves it, teaching only what has been handed on."

The doctrine of the Catholic Church has implications for exegesis.

In studying Scripture, its content and its unity, the Catholic exegete must bear in mind the living tradition of the whole Church and also, as I will explain later on, the analogy of faith. To be mindful of the living Tradition of the whole Church means first of all knowing what it is.

For the past century it seems as if scholarly exegesis has had little interest in maintaining contact with the exegesis of preceding centuries, with the exegetical tradition of the patristic age or with that of the sixteenth and seventeenth centuries, to mention only two periods particularly rich in work on Scripture. This reserve can perhaps be explained by the vast amount of work to be accomplished since the development of modern philology, and of archeology in particular—so much so that rare are the biblical works written by Catholics during the nineteenth century that would be useful to read or consult. On the contrary the impact of German scholarship, especially Protestant, was considerable. Yet today some Catholic exegetes are becoming increasingly aware that a return to the great Christian exegetical tradition would be helpful and would have a moderating effect. But we are still only taking our first faltering steps in this direction.

Again I refer for example to what has happened and is happening at the Biblical Institute. I find that a course in the history of patristic exegesis was offered from 1912 to 1934 by a most competent person in this field, namely Fr. A. Vaccari. But this course was optional. Then for thirty years, up to 1964, toward the end of the Council, no courses in patristic exegesis were offered to the students. Yet even before the Council Fr. Henri de Lubac, a man of great erudition, had taken up exegesis as it is found in the Fathers of the Church, without being himself an exegete. He published in Paris, in 1950, *Histoire et Esprit* on the exegetical writing of Origen and then especially from 1959 to 1964 his four volumes on *L'exégèse médiévale,* a monumental work that exegetes should know better. At the Institute, from 1964 on, a course was again offered every year on the work of an early Christian exegete, but it still remained optional.

Only in 1981 have our students been required to take a course on Christian exegesis in earlier centuries, on the patristic era, or on the Middle Ages or on the Renaissance period.

I believe this return to ancient Christian exegesis is of great value in linking modern Catholic exegesis to the great tradition that preceded it. This return to the patristic age is made easier by the present development in patristic studies and could very well bridge the gap that separates it from Jewish exegesis. I am thinking for example of the study made by Y. Duval of the Book of Jonah (Paris 1973) in which he shows that the exegesis proposed by Jerome (who, as is known, owed much to the Rabbis) continued right into the Middle Ages, but that it had its source in Origen who in turn had learned it from the Rabbis.

These reflections on the tradition of Christian exegesis seem important so that our way of studying the Jewish Tradition could appear in its correct light. I also wonder if the relation between Scripture and the living Tradition is not analogous to the one that exists in Judaism between the *Torah She be'alPeh,* the Oral Tradition, and the *Torah She-bikhtav,* the Written Tradition. This question deserves to be studied more closely.

C. The Analogy of Faith

Still in keeping with *Dei Verbum* (n. 12), our statutes say that exegesis must also bear in mind the analogy of faith. This expression "analogy of faith" is taken from the Apostle Paul's Epistle to the Romans (12:6), but there is controversy over its meaning. For some it means "in proportion to the faith received by the speaker"; for others it means "pertaining to the faith of the community" or "in harmony with the faith of the Church." When it is used in the context of exegetical research in the Church as has been done since Pope Leo XIII (1893), it seems to mean that when one interprets Scripture he must propound an exegesis that is in harmony with the whole of the sacred deposit of faith entrusted to the Church and therefore in harmony not only with the whole of Scripture but also with the Tradition and teaching of the Magisterium of the Church.

This formulation is not essentially restrictive (excluding what does not manifest this harmony) but rather a positive formulation which does not hamper exegetical research but situates it in its relationship to the totality of revealed truth, in the light of its responsibility to show the internal connection among the mysteries of faith.

Dei Verbum (n. 12) goes on to state: "It is the task of exegetes to work according to the rules toward a better understanding and explanation of the meaning of sacred Scripture so that through preparatory study the judgment of the Church may mature."

In the long run, it is the Church and, within the Church, its teaching office which passes judgment on the value of an exegetical work: but this exegetical work must be well-founded and properly stated, and if this is done according to the principles mentioned earlier, it will provide the Church with a better understanding of Scripture and of revealed Truth. In this way the exegete's work is a positive one.

The Catholic exegete having recourse to all available means for scholarly work such as philology, literary analysis, the study of the environment, history, archaeology, etc., and bearing in mind the unity of Scripture, the living Tradition of the whole Church and the analogy of faith, can be sure that he is faithful both to the biblical text that he is studying and to the faith of the Church, in whose service he is working; he can be sure that he is being faithful to both sound reason and his faith.

But it may be asked, "Where then is freedom of research?" Our statutes provide an answer: "Within those limits, let us grant to teachers and to scholars the freedom that is due to them and that must be used honestly and prudently according to each discipline. Consequently let what is new be proposed in such a way that continuity in truth is brought out; as for opinions, value judgments, hypotheses, which are inseparable from research, let these be proposed as such.'' Freedom of research resides "within these limits," namely those of right reason and of authentic faith; the scholarly method must be thorough and fidelity to our faith must be total.

III. QUESTIONS FOR JOINT STUDY
BY CHRISTIANS AND JEWS

The following problems need to be studied more thoroughly from a Catholic point of view, and especially in dialogue with Jewish scholars.

1. Among the questions dealing with the Old Testament to which some Catholics have already made a contribution and which need further investigation in dialogue between Jews and Catholics, I mention the following:

—the meaning and connotation of the term *Torah,* translated into Greek as *nomos* in the Septuagint, and often given as Law (cf. Laurent Monsengwo Pasinya, *La notion de Nomos dans le Pentateuque grec* [AnBib 52], Rome 1973);
—the concept and law of marriage in ancient Biblical Israel, especially as regards so-called polygamy, divorce and the role of women (cf. Angelo Tosato, *Il matrimonio israelitico. Una teoria generale* [AnBib 100], Rome 1982);
—the notion of covenant (1) in the Hebrew Bible (cf. Dennis J. McCarthy, *Treaty and Covenant* [AnBib 21A], Rome 1978; Pierre Buis, *La notion d'alliance dans l'Ancien Testament,* Paris 1976) and (2) in ancient Judaism (cf. Annie Jaubert, *La notion d'alliance dans le Judaïsme aux abords de l'ère chrétienne,* Paris 1963) (3) as related to the New Testament:
—the connection between *Ḥokma* and *Torah* in the Hebrew Bible and in intertestamental literature;
—how does the New Testament use the Hebrew Bible? (cf. Michel Gourges, *A la droite de Dieu. Résurrection de Jésus et actualisation du Psaume 110:1 dans le Nouveau Testament,* Paris 1978);

2. Pertaining to the New Testament, I suggest the following topics:

—the relationship between Torah and Gospel;
—the concept of covenant, particularly in relation to Paul's letters and the Epistle to the Hebrews;

—the Pharisees and the Sadducees at the time of Jesus and of the early Church (cf. Jean Le Moyne, *Les Sadducéens,* Paris 1972);
—the issue of the Zealots and of knowing whether Jesus can be considered a revolutionary in the political sense (cf. Hermando Guevara, *La resistencia judía contra Roma en la época de Jesús,* Meitingen 1981);
—the link between the message of Jesus and that of the Judaism of his day. The study of this question may be made easier by the fact that today Catholic exegesis shows great interest in the study of what we call the "historical Jesus";
—the trial and death of Jesus, especially on the level of responsibility: Pilate for instance (cf. Jean-Pierre Lémonon, *Pilate et le gouvernement de la Judée. Textes et monuments*, Paris 1981); the Council's declaration *Nostra aetate* has had a beneficial effect in this matter;
—the meaning of the word "Jews" in John's Gospel (cf. Johannes Beutler, in H.H. Henrix, M. Stoehr, *Exodus und Kreuz im Oekumenischen Dialog zwischen Juden und Christen* (Aachen, 1978);
—and in a general way a Catholic treatise on the Jews, using the study by Clemens Thoma, *A Christian Theology of Judaism* (New York, 1980) or by Franz Mussner, *Tractate on the Jews* (Philadelphia, 1981).

3. For the period of time following the composition of the New Testament, the following points with reference to the Bible should be studied:

—how did Christianity become separated from Judaism?
—the influence of early Jewish exegesis on patristic exegesis;
—the relation between Scripture and Tradition in the Church and in Judaism;
—how and on what principles were the canons of Scriptures in Judaism and in the Catholic Church formed?

III. MEDIEVAL HERMENEUTICS

Keep Your Sons from Scripture: The Bible in Medieval Jewish Scholarship and Spirituality

Frank Talmage

1. THE ROLE OF SCRIPTURE

The epithet "people of the book" by which the Jews have proudly styled themselves was not self-conferred. It was bestowed upon them, as it was upon Christians and Zoroastrians, by Islam to indicate their status as a people possessing an authentic pre-Quranic revelation and therefore assured of the option of retaining their ancestral religion rather than having to convert. In the case of the Jews, the "book" was the Book, the Hebrew Bible, which Israel saw itself as faithfully preserving and observing. Yet there was by no means universal consensus as to rabbinic Judaism's fidelity to the sacred text. From within, Karaism denounced Rabbanism, which was to be the prevalent form of Judaism, and its "Oral Torah" as a perversion and distortion of the entrusted revelation.[1] From without, early Christianity, in the Augustinian formulation, recognized the Jewish people as the heirs of biblical Israel and consequently entitled to continued existence as the living witness to the pre-Christian tradition. Yet, if we are to accept Jeremy Cohen's thesis, it was the thirteenth-century mendicant friars who realized that rabbinic Judaism was not at all identical with Israelite religion, and that consequently the justification for the continued existence of this heretical cult—loyal to the precepts of neither the Old nor the New Testaments—no longer held.[2]

The question we raise here, however, is not how "biblical" rabbinic Ju-

81

daism actually is, but what role the Bible played in medieval Judaism. Before broaching this question, we must note that virtually any medieval discussion of the place of independent study of Scripture will revolve around certain standard rabbinic texts. Since the variety of opinions which float in the sea of the Talmud is seemingly unlimited, the exponent of any particular point of view will find his protagonist or antagonist within it. The most positive statement on scriptural study would seem to be: "One should always divide his years into three: one third for Scripture, one third for Mishnah, and one third for Talmud" (TB *Kid.* 30a, *A.Z.* 19b).[3] The most negative and notorious is "Keep your sons from *higgayon*" (TB *Ber.* 28b), *higgayon* being understood, in many interpretations, as Scripture.[4] In between, there are a variety of statements, neither completely condemning nor overly enthusiastic, the most widely quoted being: "Engaging [lit. those who engage] in Scripture is a virtue and not a virtue [*middah ve-einah middah*, and according to some versions *middah she-einah middah*, a virtue which is no virtue];[5] in mishnah is a virtue for which one receives a reward; gemara, you have no greater virtue than this" (TB *B.M.* 33a).[6]

SEPHARDI APPROACH

Any treatment of medieval Bible study necessarily revolves around the issue of Ashkenazim vs. Sephardim. In the last centuries, until recent times, independent Bible study was neglected in the yeshivah world of central Europe and its transplants in western Europe, North America, and in the State of Israel. This Ashkenazi neglect of Scripture as Scripture and its continued cultivation among Sephardic and Oriental communities as a survival and continuation of a medieval phenomenon has become a commonplace[7] and, to be sure, does not lack documentation and justification. Throughout the centuries, we hear the plaints and complaints of Sephardim and the confessions of Ashkenazim themselves concerning Northern European neglect of the Sacred Text. In his ethical testament, Judah, the son of Asher ben Jehiel, who emigrated from Germany to Toledo with his father at the end of the thirteenth century, admonishes:

> Also appoint regular periods for study of the Bible with grammar and commentary. As in my childhood I did not study it, for in Germany they had not the custom, I have not been able to teach it here.[8]

Lamenting contemporary neglect of Scripture in turn of the fifteenth-century Spain, Profiat Duran bewails the fact that

. . . At this time I see the Sages and leading scholars of Israel neglecting Scripture. . . . If you ask them about a verse, they will not know where it is and they consider any one who spends his time on Scripture a fool for the Talmud is central. *This malady (ha-ḥoli) has been widespread in France and Germany in this and the preceding generations. . . .*[9]

Later in the fifteenth century Don Isaac Abravanel in commenting on *Ethics of the Fathers* 5:21, "Five years old for the study of Scripture, ten for the study of Mishnah," stresses that "the periods of time mentioned here refer to the *beginning* of the period of the study, not the limit. He did not say that he should engage in Scripture only *until* the age of five and not afterwards *as the Ashkenazim do today*. . . . At the age of ten he should begin Mishnah but should not stop [studying] Bible . . . [so that] he will know how to read all twenty-four books."[10]

To be sure, Mediterranean-Sephardic loyalty to biblical study cannot be gainsaid. On the basis of the survival of a plethora of biblical manuscripts and fragments in the Cairo Geniza, curricula, and so forth, S. D. Goitein has documented the centrality of biblical study from its rote learning by a child to its central place in the advanced curriculum.[11] Most telling is the testimony of R. Joseph Rosh ha-Seder in the twelfth century who listed four categories of students: ignoramuses, the broad masses (*am ha-arez*), scholars (*talmidei ḥakhamim*) and doctors (*ḥakhamim*). The broad masses knew practical Judaism, Torah and liturgy, while the scholars knew the rest of Scripture, Prophets and Writings, and halakhot. It was only the doctors, that is, decisors of the law, who were required to know mishnah, Talmud, and commentaries. Significantly then, the title *talmid ḥakham,* usually conferred upon the expert talmudist, is here associated with the biblicist.[12] But, according to the testimony of the twelfth-century traveler, Petahiah of Regensburg, even the ignorant (*am ha-arez*), i.e. the non-talmudist, was intimately familiar with Scripture in eastern lands.[13]

This tradition, if less extremely stated, continued in Islamic Spain[14] and North Africa and their cultural satellites in the Jewish world: Christian Spain and Provence.[15] Biblical and cognate philological studies were stressed as the foundation in all curricula of the period. The thirteenth-century North African Judah b. Samuel Ibn Abbas's *Ya'ir Netiv* lays out in great detail the extensive curriculum in Bible (seven and a half years) followed by grammatical study.[16] The apparently Provençal *Torah Statutes (Ḥukkei ha-Torah)* also begins its curricular program with biblical studies.[17] Most important is that we have an emphasis not only on Scripture as the foundation of Jewish learning but on its continued role throughout one's lifetime.[18] Judah ibn Tibbon in twelfth-century Lunel and his thirteenth-century compatriot, Joseph Ibn Kaspi, stress this. Whenever the latter mentions an addition to the curriculum, Bible is to be maintained.[19]

Nonetheless, one must not lose sight of the fact that Mediterranean European rabbinic Judaism in this period, no less than its Ashkenazic counterpart, was *rabbinic* Judaism, and officially, and for most, in practice, Talmud was the mainstay of the educational program. For the eleventh-century Spanish philosophical moralist, Bahya ibn Paquda, the study of Bible was clearly propaedeutic to the study of Talmud.[20] His thirteenth-century kabbalist namesake, Bahya ben Asher, leaves no doubt as to the overriding supremacy of the Oral Torah,[21] while Joseph Ezovi (Perpignan, thirteenth century) advises in his rhymed ethical testament: "Engage now in grammar, now Scripture (*pasuk*)/ But your principal concern should be with Gemara."[22] R. Meir b. Simeon ha-Meili of Narbonne in the thirteenth century makes it quite clear that while one is to spend a third of one's time on Scripture, it is to be one third and no more lest he neglect mishnah and Talmud.[23]

ASHKENAZI APPROACH

Now to be sure, no one ever accused Ashkenazi Jewry of neglecting Talmud.[24] Yet, can it be said that its total obsession for Talmud is that clear-cut? If one accepts the widely quoted dictum of Rashi's grandson Rabbenu Tam reacting to the talmudic statement that one third of one's study should be devoted to Scripture, "for us who study the Babylonian (*bavli*) Talmud, it is sufficient, for it is a composite (*balul*) of Scripture, Mishnah, and Talmud,"[25] this would appear to be the case. Rabbenu Tam's attitude toward independent Bible study seemed at best to be condescending. In the Ordinances (*takkanot*) attributed to him, one was encouraged to study Scripture only if he was not up to studying Talmud.[26] This attitude is carried over as well in the *summa* of the Ashkenazi Pietist movement, Judah the Pietist's *Sefer hasidim*.[27] Although one passage cites the rabbinic dictum about dividing one's time into thirds and even elaborating on the way this may be done, it is juxtaposed with a number of statements, which we might today call elitist, about the superiority of Talmud.[28] Further, deceptively seeming to question the rabbinic statement that the study of Scripture is a virtue and not a virtue and to state that indeed it may even be greater than the study of Talmud, it is stated that this is the case only for the ignorant (*ammei ha-arez*) who do not study Talmud, for if they did not study Scripture they would know nothing at all.[29] Indeed, the Tosaphists seemed quite content with the reduction in *Seder Rav Amram* of devoting a third of one's time (understood specifically as a third of one's day) to each of

Scripture, mishnah, and Talmud to a symbolic recitation of brief passages of each before morning prayers.[30] Nonetheless, one might examine the situation a bit more closely. Franco-German Jewry was the cultural heir of Palestinian Judaism as transmitted through Italy. Up to the first half of the tenth century, southern Italy, as reflected in the *Josippon,* as one example, relied on those texts studied in Palestine: Bible, targumim, midrashim, and mishnah. In this period, one could still be a well-educated person without being expert in the Babylonian Talmud.[31] With respect to Scripture especially, library catalogues show an abundance of Bible *(mikra)* manuscripts, *mikra* referring specifically to Prophets and Writings which, as elsewhere in the Mediterranean, was a subject for advanced study. Meshullam b. Kalonymos, a tenth-century, Italian rabbinic scholar, shows a marked biblical orientation which would now be carried over into tenth- and eleventh-century Germany.[32]

The importance of Scripture in Ashkenaz at this time might not at first be apparent because of the lack of formal biblical commentaries. Yet there are other ways of measuring concern with it. Many isolated explanations of biblical verses exist in other contexts, including verses not quoted in the Talmud showing that the biblical text was researched in it own right.[33] We find a concern with massorah (Rabbenu Gershom) and lexicology (R. Eliezer ha-Gadol),[34] as well as scriptural bias in determining halakhic decisions established by R. Leontin and reflecting a Palestinian orientation.[35] But no more eloquent testimony to familiarity with Scripture can be found than in the output of piyyut or liturgical poetry which betrays an intimate familiarity with the text of the twenty-four books, based as it is by and large on a comprehensive knowledge of the biblical lexicon.[36] The eleventh century produced R. Jacob b. Yakar, styled "teacher of gemara and Scripture *(mikra),*" the teacher of Rashi who clearly inaugurated a glorious era in Ashkenazi biblical studies.[37] This is not the place to evaluate the nature of Rashi's biblical commentaries, nor those of his allegedly more "rationalistic" disciples and members of his school, Joseph Kara, Joseph Bekhor Shor, Samuel ben Meir (Rashbam), son of Rashi's son-in-law, Meir b. Samuel, himself hardly ignorant of Scripture, Eliezer of Beaugeney, and others.[38] The fact is that Ashkenazi biblicism—*pace* Rabbenu Tam (who in fact himself wrote a commentary on Job and was no mean philologist, devoting an entire work to the controversy between the tenth-century Spanish grammarians Menahem ben Saruk and Dunash ibn Labrat)—was all-pervasive in this period, the search for the "plain" sense of Scripture *(peshateh di-Kera)* being found among the tosafists themselves.[39]

The attitude of twelfth-century Ashkenazi biblicism is well expressed in two interpretations of "Keep your sons from Scripture." Rashi in his commentary *ad locum* comments "Do not let them become too accustomed to Scripture (*mikra*) because it draws (*mi-shum de-mashekhah*) [them away from other study]."[40] Samuel b. Meir harmonizes the talmudic text with Rashi's explanation and quotes: "Do not allow your sons too much (*al tarbu*) Scripture." For R. Samuel the rabbinic proscriptions of *Ber.* 28b and *Kid.* 30a are not a warrant against studying Scripture but against studying it divorced from its midrashic interpretations. All this, as far as R. Samuel was concerned, because of their piety![41] But clearly a less "pious" age had been inaugurated by Rashi and the time for looking at Scripture qua Scripture (*peshuto shel mikra*) had arrived. Indeed, the new biblicism was even to be found among the very German Pietists who, at our initial glance at the *Sefer hasidim,* seemed lukewarm toward independent study of the Sacred Text. This is seen in a striking passage in the commentary to the liturgy of Eleazar of Worms, a foremost disciple of Judah the Pietist.

> It is good to know Scripture for we learn many commandments from the prophetic writings (*ha-kabbalah*). . . . Now [because] there may be no prophecy in our meditation day and night on Psalms, Job, Proverbs, Ezra, and the Scrolls . . . by which we may succeed in knowing a commandment by virtue of which we will inherit the life of the World to Come, [and] the Sages said concerning the study of Scripture that it is a virtue and not a virtue, it is yet good for the scholar (*maskil*) that he fathom the nature of the Holy Tongue from Scripture. . . . It is not proper for the cultivated scholar (*la-navon ha-maskil*) to lack a knowledge of Scripture, for when it is stated in the Talmud "it is said," he will not know in what book it is said, [or] if it is so according to the plain sense (*peshat*), or midrash, or simply a scriptural support (*asmakhta*), and he who does not know Scripture will not know how to read the verse. . . .[42]

R. Eleazar's words were not original. They are based on a passage in the Spanish biblicist and savant Abraham Ibn Ezra's *Yesod mora,*[43] in which he critically categorizes various types of scholars; while warning the biblical scholars that Scripture cannot be understood outside of the context of rabbinic tradition, he admonishes the talmudist that rabbinic tradition is based on Scripture. The *Yesod mora* was written in England, a part, culturally and spiritually, of the French sphere of influence, and Ibn Ezra's critique may be seen as a direct address to Ashkenazi talmudists. The fact that Eleazar of Worms himself incorporates it into his writings as a corrective to those who would be extreme in their neglect of independent study of the Bible is one demonstration that the matter was not so one-sided. Indeed, it was the very strength of Ashkenazi biblicism in the twelfth and thirteenth centuries that made its weakening in the fourteenth century all the more lamentable to one such as Profiat Duran.[44]

The distinction made then between Ashkenazim and Sephardim would seem to be based on the choice of criteria for the determination of what constitutes biblicism, principally the inclusion of biblical study as a formal part of the curriculum in the same way it was articulated in Spain. A fuller picture is obtained by allowing the many other witnesses to bear testimony. One may, of course, raise the question of whether Ashkenazi biblical learning was the property of only a select few or was more generalized, but one can ask too to what extent the Sephardi curricula reflect the program of an elite or of the masses.

Be this as it may, there does indeed seem to be a decline in biblical study in the fourteenth century among Ashkenazim (and according to Duran's testimony among Sephardim as well). What might the cause of this have been? One possible answer is in accord with the so-called "lachrymose" conception of Jewish history according to which the tribulations and sufferings of Ashkenazi Jewry limited their capacity for study and caused, according to the sixteenth-century Bohemian scholar, Hayyim b. Bezalel (brother of Maharal of Prague), complaining of the lack of philological studies in his time, "our sainted forefathers, and in particular the Ashkenazi pietists, to direct their sons to Talmud alone and to train them and educate them according to this holy book. . . ."[45] This statement follows the well-known rationalization of Natronai Gaon for neglect in his own time of the talmudic principle that one is required to divide one's time into three, devoting one third to Scripture: "since poverty and indigence have increased and scholars have had to earn a living from their own labor and not spend all their time on Torah . . . they depended on the Talmud alone and neglected Bible and mishnah, relying on their statement:[46] All streams run to the sea (Eccl. 1:7) Scripture, mishnah and midrash."[47] Yet just as B. Z. Dinur questioned this socio-economic explanation of Natronai ascribing the increased stress on Talmud to modifications in the educational system,[48] we may suggest that attitudes toward curriculum had their origins elsewhere.

We should note first that in the Mediterranean-Sephardic world curricular expansion led to a restriction on biblical studies as well. In Maimonides' expansive formulations of the third-third-third dictum, in which he incorporates metaphysics or esoteric studies into the portion of study designated as Talmud, he notes that after the initial period of study when one "no longer needs to learn the Written Law . . . he should, at fixed times, rend the Written Law and the traditional dicta, so as not to forget any of the rules of the Torah, and should devote all his days exclusively to the study of Talmud, according to his breadth of mind and maturity of intellect."[49] Echoes of this are heard even in Profiat Duran who notes that with the necessity of studying secular sciences, it is permitted to follow a four-fold rather than a three-fold curriculum once one reached ethical and spiritual maturity.[50] Second, we may observe a similar phenomenon in the world of the Christian universities.

With the introduction of Peter Lombard's *Sentences* as the second "set text" after the Bible in the twelfth century, the disciplines of theology and Bible study became differentiated. At first the *Sentences* were taught in the context of reliance on Sacred Scripture, and indeed the twelfth and certainly the thirteenth century may be seen as a golden age of medieval Christian biblical exegesis.[51] Yet by the fourteenth century commentators on the *Sentences* turned increasingly to philosophy and theology, paying, as Beryl Smalley notes, less attention to Bible in practice though maintaining its primacy in theory.[52] In brief, an expanded curriculum requires that something be lost.[53] If we look at the Talmud then as our second set text and its study and cultivation as the counterpart of theology, we see roughly the same process. And it should not surprise us then to find that the fourteenth century return to Scripture, as expressed in the thinking of Wyclif and Hus, corresponds to a similar reaction in Judaism on the part of Profiat Duran[54] in Catalonia as well as of pivotal Ashkenazi figures in Bohemian Judaism to whom we shall soon turn.

THE QUALITY OF BIBLICAL STUDY:
LOW MIDDLE AGES

The questions that we have posed, namely the reasons for the ebbs and flows in explicit emphasis on Scripture in either the Sephardi or Ashkenazi traditions and the actual extent of that emphasis measured quantitatively, are questions which are of primary importance to the contemporary biblical exegete or historian of exegesis working in a critical academic framework, whether in a university or seminary context. The latter is more often than not interested in medieval exegesis and Bible study only to the degree that they can serve as a prototype for the kind of work he himself is doing, and to the degree that the roots of modern biblical criticism, higher and lower, can be found among the medievals.[55] Yet where the historian of religion approaches the question of the place of Scripture in medieval Judaism, the critical exegetical and quantitative aspects lose their primacy.

The question that comes to the fore now is the qualitative nature of biblical study—whether independent or in conjunction with rabbinic tradition—that is, what role did it play not only in science but in spirituality? When we examine our classic "scientific" curricula, we find that the biblical and cognate philological studies are frequently seen as a rung on the ladder to theological enlightenment and not as a pursuit *in vacuo*. Joseph Kimhi, exegete and philologist par excellence, stresses this in the introduction to his work on lexicography, the *Sefer ha-galui*,[56] while his confrere, the Lunel translator, Judah Ibn Tibbon, juxtaposes the reading of Scripture with the reading of ethical works, chief of which is Proverbs,[57] in his admonition to his son Samuel.[58] And Ibn Tibbon, that classic Lear of medieval Judaism, who constantly bewails his son's infidelity to his ideals (documented only by Judah's self-pity but nowhere by Samuel's actual deeds), admonishes the latter to "look at the chapter concerning Jonadab son of Rechab every Sabbath, to instil in thee diligence to fulfil my commands."[59]

In other words, the principal purpose of Bible study is edification of some sort. Thus, the plaint of Samuel Ibn Tibbon's son-in-law, Jacob Anatoli, the thirteenth-century homilist, on the reading of Scripture is hardly atypical. Decrying those who utter prayers without paying attention to their meaning, he continues that

> when we read the words of the prophets which were undoubtedly written with great purposes, we read only occasionally as [one would read] old wives' tales. Also [if we are to speak of] the books of the sage Solomon whose purpose is to alert us to save ourselves from all these pitfalls, we read two of his books once a year [Song of Songs at Passover, and Ecclesiastes at Tabernacles] and that reading is like the reading of a history book. As for the third [Proverbs], we read it once in a lifetime, and that as if it were a poem.[60]

If we keep in mind that old wives' tales, histories, and poetry were hardly among the most esteemed literary genres in the eyes of many a thirteenth-century Maimonidean, we get the point rather easily. Yet perhaps the most eloquent statement on the spiritual value of the reading of the Scriptures is found once again in the introduction to a grammar, the *Maaseh efod,* of the turn of the fifteenth-century Catalonian, Profiat Duran.[61]

Grammar, we must recall, was considered indispensable to an understanding of Scripture, but the true purpose of the study of Scripture becomes clear from Duran's exposition. He begins with a three-fold classification of Jewish scholarship—talmudism, philosophy, and kabbalah—finding merit in each but rejecting any one claim to complete hegemony. The study of Talmud is a noble enterprise indeed since it is a true intellectual exercise, and, in the Maimonidean world, intellectual perfection is the guarantor of the World-to-Come. Through a remarkable sleight-of-hand, Duran equates the highest level of metaphysician, said to be in the inner court with the King in Maimonides' *Guide* 3:71, with the most sophisticated type of talmudist (*Maaseh efod*, p. 8). Yet despite this high praise, there are those talmudists who make a fundamental error—the claim to exclusivity[62] and this, for Duran, is unpardonable when the exclusion is Bible.[63] Duran refers to the fact that their rationalization that any study of Scripture—Torah, Prophets, and Writings—is a "waste of time" is based on the rabbinic statement

> which says—according to some versions—[For] those who engage in Scripture, it is a virtue and not a virtue (*middah ve-einah middah*) (TB *B.M.* 33a) and on their saying "Keep your sons from Scripture" (TB *Ber.* 28b) which Rashi explained: "Do not make them too accustomed to Scripture (*mikra*) because it draws [one]."

Duran, however, ingeniously proceeds to explain this classic apparently anti-scriptural statement away by reconciling it with the text from TB *Kid.* 30a.

But this is not so because the Sages of blessed memory said: One should always divide one's time into three—a third for

> Scripture, a third for Mishnah, a third for Talmud. [Consequently] Rashi meant by "too [accustomed]" *more* than the allotted third. Perish the thought that one of the sages of the Talmud would think that engaging in Scripture was worthless (*ibid.*, p. 6).

Later, Duran makes another attempt, based on older tradition, to reexplain "Keep your sons from *higgayon*" so that *higgayon* does not mean Scripture but superficial reading.[64] *Higgayon* is a homonym said of what they read without concentration as in "[they] that chirp and mutter (*ha-mahgim*, from the same root as *higgayon*) (Isa. 8:19)" (*ibid.*, p. 19).[65]

If this is the case though, it may strike one initially as surprising that even mechanical reading of Scripture is considered meritorious, although to be sure true research into its meaning is more so (*ibid.*, pp. 13–14).

> "This book of the Torah shall not depart out of your mouth but you shall read (*ve-hagita*) therein day and night" (Jos. 1:8). The wonder is that he said "You shall read" for *hagiyyah* which is reading (*keriah*) is something which will bring about [beatitude], especially if it is with proper understanding of its intention, the comprehension of its mysteries and secrets . . . (*ibid.*, p. 10).

For Duran, engaging in Scripture then is meritorious at any level and at the highest level it is the supreme activity: "true worship (*avodah*) of God is engaging in the Torah and the Prophets, researching and scrutinizing them" (*ibid.*, p. 14). So great are the words of Scripture—of Bible not Talmud—that

> He commanded that they be frontlets between their eyes, that they be bound on the hands and written on the doorposts. *Now this is said concerning that which is written in the Torah not that which was handed down through tradition which is the Oral Torah,* and because of the fear that occupation with the written Torah might diminish because of the study of [oral] tradition, it was not to be written down as they said "That which is transmitted orally you are not allowed to put in writing" (TB *Git.* 60b), because it was feared that this might be a cause of diversification of views and opinions and a proliferation of controversies. From this would follow a diminishing of occupation [with the written Torah]. Because of this they said, " 'He caused me to dwell in dark places' (Lam. 3:b). This [refers to] the Babylonian Talmud" (cf. TB *San.* 28a) (*ibid.*, p. 10; cf. p. 14).

Yet despite Duran's estimation of Scripture—an estimation faintly reminiscent of the contemporary Wyclifite and Hussite call for a return to Scripture—he does not establish a fourth school of biblicists alongside the first three of talmudists, philosophers, and kabbalists. Rather, if we examine the structure of his text, we note that the entire discussion of biblicism flows out of and is intertwined with his discussion of kabbalism. For the fact is that for Duran, the value of occupation with Scripture is not primarily intellectual but theurgic, the reading (*hagiyyah*) and engagement (*esek*) with it "drawing down the divine effulgence (*shefa*) in order that divine providence cleave to the nation by virtue of the inherent power (*segullah*) cleaving to the words of the Torah. . . . And if what is said of the [Divine] Names and the Torah being full of them is true,[66] this will confirm [our] view (*ibid.*, p. 10; cf. p. 13)." Duran reiterates that it is precisely the study of Scripture "which has caused this drawing down of the divine effulgence and the immediate cause of the maintenance and survival of the notion in the time of this long exile through the inherent power which cleaves to it" (*ibid.*, p. 11).

There are two further important aspects to this. One is that any scripturally related activity is seen as having a special merit even if it be something which on the surface is purely technical such as the study of massorah and indeed of grammar (Duran, *Maaseh efod*, p. 13). Indeed, Duran's own composition of the *Maaseh efod*, a biblical grammar, is seen not as a simple scholarly task but has apocalyptic overtones (*ibid.*, p. 128). Knowledge of Scripture can not be fragmentary; it must be read until known by heart (*ibid.*, p. 17).

The second important aspect is that the numinous quality of Scripture is not confined to the Torah alone but characterizes all twenty-four books of the canon. For Duran, the entire Bible is the surviving "Temple of God" (*mikdash Yah*).[67] Just as the Temple was divided into three sections, the holy of holies, the sanctuary, and the outer court in accord with the three worlds—upper, intermediate, and lower—so is the Bible divided into three parts in accord with three levels of sanctity (*ibid.*, p. 11).

Now despite the fact that there is a descending order of holiness, and a priority of order and study, for Duran there is a special place for the Writings precisely because they correspond to this world. Even though Lamentations, for example, is properly a prophetic book, it is assigned to the Writings because of its theme of the Temple (*ibid.*). It should not surprise us then that the Book of Psalms, in its entirety and in the passages recited in the liturgy, occupies a very special role in Duran's program (*ibid.*, p. 10). He goes so far as to blame the neglect of the Bible, the study of which was originally as strong as that of Talmud (*ibid.*, p. 13), on the part of Ashkenazi Jews in the fourteenth century for their troubles and persecutions (for it is as if they neglected the Temple service itself), while he maintains that to the extent that the communities of Aragon and Catalonia were saved in the persecutions of 1391–92, it was because of their praying and reading of Scripture and especially of the Book of Psalms—not intellectual study but devotional reading which, in the kabbalistic usage of *shimmushei tehillim* to which he refers, has theurgic potency (*ibid.*, p. 10).

Now it is of some significance that this stress on the salvific quality of Psalm reading[68] is not confined to the Sephardic world alone. At the end of his commentary to Psalm 150, Avigdor Kara of Prague, a technical Bible scholar,[69] relates a remarkable story in this regard. Because of its intrinsic interest and its demonstration of the role of Psalm reading in popular religion, we may cite it in full here:

Know that I heard from my sainted and martyred father in the year 1351, two years after the persecutions [accompanying the Black Death], that there was a village near Erfurt which was not overtaken by the adversaries. There was a poor, pious person, who knew little other than the literal sense of Scripture, living there. He was old and died of natural causes at a ripe old age. Within thirty days after his death, he came and revealed him to an outstanding and pious scholar who lived in Erfurt, and it seemed to him that he was standing before him in his shrouds with a small book under his arm. Then the pious man said to him: "Aren't you the man we buried here on such-and-such a day?" He said to him: "You have spoken correctly. I am he." He said to him: "What's that book you have?" He said to him: "It is the Book of Psalms and I have come to advise you to warn the people of the community in which I lived that they flee from the city and save their lives since they are destined for evil and must flee to [other] communities. "For all the while I was alive, I completely recited the Book of Psalms twice every day, and because of that they lived in peace for a long time and were saved up to now. But now they have no one to defend them." In the morning, the pious man became agitated and sent a special [message] in his own hand to warn them. Now those who feared the words of the pious man escaped and were saved and others who despaired of the retribution remained there and did not heed the word of the pious man so that the hand of God and His judgment struck them. And from the day that my sainted father heard this, he did not neglect saying Psalms every day. . . ."[70]

THE QUALITY OF BIBLICAL STUDY: RENAISSANCE

While we thus see a fusion of science and spirituality in this period, it is of interest to look briefly at two other writers who lived approximately two centuries after Duran when the Middle Ages and the Renaissance were yet indistinct. This was the age of Don Isaac Abravanel, the illustrious leader of pre- and post-Expulsion Jewry, whose own biblical scholarship was no less than prodigious and whose critique of Ashkenazi neglect of Scripture in his time we have seen above. In the world of an Abravanel and his confreres, one may be initially surprised to see his fellow Iberian and younger contemporary, Joseph Hayyun, active in Lisbon[71] in the period before the Expulsion, seemingly "revert" to the stereotypical "Ashkenazi" position. In commenting on *Ethics of the Fathers* 5:21 with which we are familiar, Hayyun observes:

. . . At the age of five he is fit to study Scripture—Torah, Prophets, Writings—in which he should persist five years until the age of ten. They should not be trained in Scripture more than this, for occupation with Scripture is a virtue which is no virtue (*middah she-einah middah*) and they said further "Keep your sons from Scripture" . . .
Now I think that one of the reasons that our learning has deteriorated (*avedah hokhmatenu*) in our time is that students have been overly trained in Scripture during their youth and if they were trained in Gemara during their youth as this sage has ordered, they would gain in wisdom. . . .
"Fifteen years for Gemara" . . . At this age and henceforth he will spend all his time at Gemara. And even though they said "One should always divide one's years into three, etc.," Rabbenu Tam explained that study of Gemara includes all three. . . .[72]

One might consider this merely an aberration from Sephardic biblicism,[73] if it were not for the fact that Hayyun himself, like Abravanel, was a biblical scholar. His commentary to Psalms was published in Salonika in 1522 and commentaries to other biblical books are said to exist in manuscript.[74] It may be instructive to compare Hayyun's words with those of a slightly later contemporary and compatriot, Joseph Garçon, who had his origins in Castile but lived in Portugal and then after the Expulsion in Salonika and elsewhere in the East. An ambitious homilist, Garçon was no stranger to sacred Scripture. Yet in expounding on Isa. 65:13, he observes:

> Everyone receives his portion in the World. Therefore [we have] this parable. Concerning those who have occupied themselves with Scripture it is said: "Behold, My servants shall eat," for eating is a coarse function and also one who knows Scripture alone is not worthy of a great reward. . . . "Behold, My servants shall drink" refers to those who have studied Talmud for that is refined. Just as drinking is more refined than eating they will have a higher status in the World to Come. . . . Of those who have studied kabbalistic theology or have attained the rank of prophecy which is true joy for they know and apprehend their Lord, it is said "Behold, My servants shall rejoice" . . .[75]

RECONCILIATION OF OPPOSITES

The positions of Hayyun and Garçon are at first blush a reversal of that of Duran, but in reality we may question if they are not two sides of the same coin. For Duran, one of the last medieval biblical grammarians of note, critical biblical study is of paramount importance because it is at the root of the theological enterprise; its study clearly had a redemptive aspect. The disparaging of critical biblical study which we seem to see in Hayyun and Garçon should be paradoxical in figures intimately familiar with Scripture and schooled in medieval philology.[76] What they in fact might be eschewing is the phenomenon of the divorcing of scriptural scholarship from its theological context and spiritual dimension. This is the same dilemma and the same tension that is encountered among both Ashkenazim and Sephardim throughout the Middle Ages. But this was a creative tension which produced in various forms and guises scholars who could make that which was apparently contradictory complementary. In this, they were worthy models for their latter-day disciples who know how to use their teachings with discretion.

Preliminary Note

NOTE: Before embarking on this paper, I was under the impression that a similar study already existed. Since I failed to locate it, I proceeded with my work. On the very morning that I was finishing this piece, Prof. Herbert Basser of Queen's University reminded me, to my embarrassment, that Moshe Idel referred to Mordecai Breuer, "Keep Your Children from *Higgayon*" [Hebrew] in *Mikhtam le-David: Sefer zikhron ha-rav David Ochs,* eds. Yitshak Gilat and Eliezer Stern (Ramat-Gan, 1978), pp. 242–64 in his own comments on the subject in his "On the History of the Interdiction against the Study of Kabbalah before the Age of Forty" [Hebrew], *AJSreview* 5 (1980): 15–20 (Heb. sec.). Prof. Breuer's article is characterized by his customary mastery of the material and insight. Inevitably, we were led to many of the same sources and observations. However, our focus and perspectives do differ somewhat. Where Prof. Breuer deals with certain points in greater detail than I felt necessary here, I have referred the reader to his article in the notes. My thanks to Prof. Basser for this and other bibliographical references and to the Social Sciences and Humanities Research Council of Canada for their support of a project on medieval biblical exegesis in conjunction with which this paper was written.

NOTES

1. Although the Bible in Karaite Judaism lies outside the purview of this essay, it may be questioned whether Karaism was in fact more biblically oriented than rabbinic Judaism since Scripture may well have been exegeted in conformity with actual sectarian practice. See Zvi Ankori, *Karaites in Byzantium* (New York and Jerusalem, 1959), pp. 209–10.

2. See Jeremy Cohen, *The Friars and the Jews* (Ithaca and London, 1982).

3. The literature is replete with discussions of how this division was to be undertaken, as portions of a day or a week or in sequences of years. See, e.g., Tosafot, *Kid.* 30a, s.v. *lo.* This, however, is not pertinent for our purposes. It should be noted, however, that since this is a dictum of Joshua b. Hananiah (first century), Talmud here does not refer to the Babylonian or Palestinian Talmuds but to the students' own analytical research. The medievals, however, generally understood this as a reference to the Babylonian Talmud, although Maimonides came strikingly close to the original meaning of the text. See Hil. Talmud Torah 1:11–12 and the discussion thereof in Isadore Twersky, *Introduction to the Code of Maimonides* (Mishneh Torah) (New Haven and London, 1980), pp. 484–95.

4. See Rashi, *ad loc.*: "Do not make them overly accustomed to Scripture *(mikra)* . . ."; *ʿArukh,* s.v. *hg:* "from the interpretation *(pitron)* of the verse in its face

meaning (*ke-ṣurato*)." On the possible original meanings of *higgayon* in this context, see Saul Lieberman, *Hellenism in Jewish Palestine* (New York, 1962), pp. 103, 108–9 and notes; Naphtali Wieder, *The Judean Scrolls and Karaism* (London, 1962), pp. 216–39, esp. 236–39. While Wieder basically accepts the original meaning of *higgayon* as Rashi and the ᶜ*Arukh* understood it, Lieberman is inclined to see it as logic and dialectics and adduces several medieval sources in support. While it is important for us to realize that the equation *higgayon* = *mikra* was not universally accepted in the Middle Ages, it should be noted that *higgayon* as logic in *medieval* usage is based on an Arabism (*mantik* = logic). This interpretation transfers the Talmudic text from its role in the controversy over the study of Bible to one in the dispute over the study of philosophy. See the attribution of this to R. Hai Gaon in Abba Mari Moses Astruc, *Minḥat kenaot* (Pressburg, 1838), no. 93, p. 172; and Samuel Ibn Tibbon, *Perush ha-millot ha-zarot*, s.v. *higgayon*. See also the commentary of Simeon b. Zemah Duran to *Ethics of the Fathers, Magen avot* (Jerusalem, 1960/61), p. 87: "Keep your children from *higgayon* is not *al-mantik*," and Breuer, "Keep," pp. 246–47 and notes. Breuer deals at length with this aspect in his study.

5. *Dikdukei soferim* does not record these variants, but the sources have not only *ve-eino* and *she-eino* but a harmonizing *ve-she-eino*. The two major variants are apparently due to preferences of geographic provenance and have no semantic significance, the expression meaning "somewhat of a virtue" (cf. Rashi *ad. loc.*).

6. See the texts cited in Simhah ben Samuel of Vitry. *Maḥzor Vitry*, ed. S. Hurwitz (Nürnberg, 1923), no. 524, chap. 16, pp. 709–11 and in B.-Z. Dinur, *Yisrael ba-golah*, 2d rev. and enl. ed. (Tel Aviv and Jerusalem, 1958–), vol. 1, bk. 4 (1962), pp. 40–46. Cf. also *Yalkut ha-makhiri to Psalms* (Jerusalem, 1964), p. 3a. The texts cited by Dinur imply that Bible was to be studied in the context of its rabbinic interpretation. According to him, the rabbis found this necessary because of the contradiction between the biblical world and contemporary reality which the rabbinic interpretations would "smooth over" (*meṭayyehim*) (p. 46, n. 38).

7. See H. J. Zimmels, *Ashkenazim and Sephardim* (London, 1958), pp. 146–47.

8. Israel Abrahams, *Hebrew Ethical Wills*, 1 vol. in 2 (Philadelphia, 1926), p. 174. It should be noted though that R. Judah's admonition is in the context of clear stress on the overriding importance of talmudic and halakhic study.

9. Profiat Duran, *Maaseh efod*, ed. Jonathan Friedlaender (Vienna, 1865), p. 41 and see below. Duran is echoing the complaint of Isaac Ibn Latif in the preceding century. See introduction to *Shaar ha-shamayim*, in *He-ḥaluẓ* 12 (1887):121.

10. *Pirkei avot . . . im perush Naḥalat avot* (Jerusalem 1969/70), p. 371.

11. S. D. Goitein, *Sidrei ḥinnukh* (Jerusalem, 1962), pp. 18, 53, 138; *idem, A Mediterranean Society*, 3 vols. (Berkeley, Los Angeles and London, 1971), 2:182, 184, 206.

12. Goitein, *Sidrei ḥinnukh*, p. 42; *Mediterranean Society*, pp. 265–66.

13. Petahiah ben Jacob, *Sibbuv ha-rav rabbi Petahiah mi-Regensburg*, ed. L. Grünhut (Frankfurt am Main, 1905), p. 8.

14. Cf. the statement of the eleventh century Saragossan, Johan Ibn Janah (*Sefer ha-rikmah*, ed. Mordecai Wilenski, 2d ed., 2 vols. [Jerusalem, 1964], 1: 10–16). While Ibn Janah is frequently touted as a champion of biblical learning, he was in fact primarily concerned with grammatical study which he saw as necessary for *both* biblical and talmudic study. He did, however, insist, against the talmudists, that Scripture be allowed its own integrity and that interpretations based on sound philology and independent of rabbinic interpretation be accredited, especially since the rabbis themselves recognized the validity of this approach.

15. Indeed, it is Talmud that may get short shrift. Cf. the twelfth-century exile to North Africa, Judah Ibn Aknin, in *Tibb al-nufus,* in Mortiz Guedemann, *Das jüdische Unterrichtswesen während der Spanisch-Arabischen Periode* (Vienna, 1873), pp. 54–58 (German), p. 8 (Arabic).

16. Guedemann, *Unterrichtswesen,* pp. 144–48 (German), p. 58 (Arabic).

17. Cited from Simḥah Assaf, *Mekorot le-toledot ha-ḥinnukh be-yisra'el,* 4 vols. (Tel Aviv and Jerusalem, 1925–42), 1:15.

18. Abrahams, *Wills,* p. 82.

19. See, e.g., Abrahams, *Wills,* p. 144.

20. Baḥya Ibn Paquda, *Ḥovot ha-levavot,* 3:4.

21. Baḥya ben Asher, *Kad ha-kemaḥ,* s.v. *torah* 1, ed. C. B. Chavel, *Kitvei rabbenu Baḥya* (Jerusalem, 1969/70), p. 422.

22. Assaf, *Mekorot,* 2:49.

23. Meir ben Simeon ha-Meili, *Sefer ha-meorot,* ed. M. Y. Blau (New York, 1966), p. 94. In general see Frank Talmage, *David Kimhi: The Man and the Commentaries* (Cambridge, Mass. and London, 1975), pp. 9–14 and Breuer, "Keep," pp. 248–49.

24. See Zimmels, *Ashkenazim and Sephardim,* ibid.; Breuer, "Keep," pp. 249–51.

25. See *Tosafot* to TB *A.Z.* 19b, s.v. *yeshallesh* based on TB *San.* 24a: "What is Babylonia *(Bavel)*? A composite *(belulah)* of Scripture, a composite of Mishnah, a composite of Talmud." The *Tosafot* to that passage quote R. Tam as saying "By virtue of our Talmud, we are exempted from the statement of the sages that one should divide his years into three."

26 Assaf, *Mekorot,* 1:4.

27. *Sefer ḥasidm,* ed. Jehuda Wistinetzki, 2d. ed. (Frankfurt am Main, 1924), no. 825, p. 209.

28. *Ibid.,* no. 790, p. 200.

29. *Ibid.,* no. 765, p. 193; cf. no. 824, p. 209.

30. *Tosafot,* San. 24a, s.v. *belulah;* Kid. 30a, s.v. *lo.* However, it must be noted that *Seder Rav Amram* itself notes that "this is the custom of all Israel in Spain." *Oẓar ha-geonim,* Kid. (vol. 9), *Teshuvot,* p. 82.

31. Roberto Bonfil, "Tra Due Mondi: Prospettive di Ricerca sulla Storia Culturale degli Ebrei nell'Italia Meridionale nell'Alto Medioevo," *Italia Judaica* (1983): 155–57.

32. *Ibid.*, pp. 151–53.

33. Avraham Grossman, *Ḥakhmei Ashkenaz ha-rishonim* (Jerusalem, 1981), p. 419.

34. *Ibid.*, pp. 160–61.

35. *Ibid.*, pp. 430–32. In principle, halakhah could be derived only from the Pentateuch, but this had already been connived at in rabbinic times. See E. E. Urbach, *Ḥazal: Pirkei emunot ve-deot* (Jerusalem, 1969), p. 255.

36. *Ibid.*, p. 419; Urbach, ed., Abraham ben Azriel, *Arugat ha-bosem*, 4 vols. (Jerusalem, 1963), 4:150–54. On evidence of familiarity with Scripture through poetical texts, cf. Beryl Smalley, "L'exégèse biblique dans la littérature latine," *La Bibbia nell'Alto Medioevo (Settimane di Studio del Centro Italiano di Studi Sull'Alto Medioevo*, (Spoleto, 1963), pp. 631–56.

37. Grossman, *Ḥakhmei Ashkenaz*, p. 240.

38. See E. E. Urbach, *Baalei ha-tosafot*, 1 vol. in 2, 4th enl. ed. (Jerusalem, 1980), pp. 44–48. On the Franco-German school of exegetes, see Moshe Greenberg, ed. *Parshanut ha-miqra ha-yehudit* (Jerusalem, 1983) (reprinted from the *Enziklopedyah mikrait*), pp. 68–86 and the bibliography listed there; E. I. J. Rosenthal, "The Study of the Bible in Medieval Judaism" (*Cambridge History of the Bible = CHB*), 3 vols. (Cambridge, 1969), 2:260–66 and bibliography on pp. 521–22.

39. Urbach, *Baalei ha-tosafot*, pp. 333, 340 and in general, index, s.v. *parshanut ha-mikra yehudit*. See also the anonymous commentary to *Ethics of the Fathers* in *Maḥzor Vitry,*, p. 324. With reference to R. Tam, it is interesting to see the perspective of his Hispano-Provençal critic Joseph Kimhi, in *Sefer ha-galui* (ed. H. J. Mathews [Berlin, 1887]), p. 2: "he did not make an effort at grammar . . . and not occupy himself with Scripture *(higgayon)* because it is a virtue and not a virtue."

40. There is a long tradition that the prohibition against *higgayon* was due to the possibility that a reading of Scripture, or at least a superficial reading, could lead to heresy. See the statement of Zemah b. Paltoi Gaon, *Oẓar ha-geonim*, Berakhot (vol. 1), *Perushim*, p. 40 from Abraham Zacut, *Sefer yuḥasin*, ed. Herschell Filipowski, p. 124: "from *higgayon*: from reading Scriptural texts *(la-hagot ba-mikraot)* because they tend to heresy." On the basis of this, some have contended that Rashi's original text read "mi-shum de-mashekha le-minut (because it draws one to heresy)" (Wieder, *Judean Scrolls*, p. 238, n. 4) but this is questionable (cf. Breuer, "Keep," p. 244, n. 10). Menahem ha-Meiri apparently read the interpretation of the ᶜ*Arukh* in terms of the possibility of the study of Scripture leading to heresy: "One must educate [one's sons] from childhood not to interpret *(liftor)* a verse literally *(ke-ṣurato)* in any way that its plain meaning *(peshuto)* supports any kind of disbelief" (*Beit ha-beḥirah*, ed. Shmuel Dikman [Jerusalem, 1959/60], p. 101. The fear of Bible study outside the context of rabbinic tradition is expressed too by Judah b. Barzilay in his Commentary to *Sefer Yesirah* (Berlin, 1885), p. 6, who states that "many biblicists whom we see today are close to being heretics since they do not know Talmud and the interpretations of the commandments," and cf. Breuer, "Keep," p. 248, n. 26. In the northern European context, heresy here came to mean Christianity

with the Church charging that Jewish knowledge of the Scriptures would lead to their conversion. For a clear statement, see Innocent IV in Solomon Grayzel, *The Church and the Jews in the XIIIth Century*, rev. ed. (New York, 1966), pp. 250–53, and in Gregory IX's letter, appended to the decree against the Talmud in the context of the Disputation of Paris, Chen Merchavia, *Ha-Talmud bi-rei ha-nazrut* (Jerusalem, 1970), p. 258 (citing Ber. 28a and B.M. 33a). See in greater detail, Breuer, "Keep," p. 250 and in general, pp. 246–48.

41. Comm. to Gen. 37:1, ed. David Rosin (Breslau, 1881/82), p. 49.
42. Cited in Urbach, *Arugat ha-bosem*, 4:111.
43. Abraham Ibn Ezra, *Yesod mora* (Jerusalem, 1930/31), pp. 1–2.
44. Duran, *Maaseh efod*, p. 41.
45. In his introduction to *ᶜEz hayyim*, cited in Assaf, *Mekorot*, 1:44.
46. S.S. Rabbah 12:5, Mid. Mishlei 10:16.
47. Jacob Mussafia, ed. *Teshuvot ha-geonim* (Lyck, 1864), no. 9, p. 28b. See *Mahzor Vitry*, no. 47, p. 26; Breuer, "Keep," p. 248, n. 25.
48. Dinur, *Yisrael ba-golah*, pt. 1, bk. 4, p. 426, no. 40. Hayyim b. Bezalel's brother, Maharol (Judah b. Loew) saw the cause for neglect of Bible study in the exaggerated emphasis on *pilpul* (casuistic Talmud study). See Breuer, "Keep," pp. 258–60. This, however, is beyond the scope of this essay.
49. M.T. *Hil. Talmud Torah* 1:12; Isadore Twersky, *Introduction to the Code of Maimonides* (Mishneh Torah) (New Haven and London, 1980), p. 489 and ensuing discussions.
50. Duran, *Maaseh efod*, p. 17.
51. Smalley, "Bible," p. 206.
52. *Ibid.*, p. 199 and cf. the formulation of Goitein, *Med. Soc.*, 2:206.
53. Smalley, "Bible," p. 202.
54. See Frank Talmage, *Kitvei pulmos le-Profiat Duran* (Jerusalem, 1981), p. 10. One point of contact between Jewish and Wyclifite and Hussite emphasis on Scripture is that both maintained Scripture was to be read in the context of tradition. One did not have here the *Scriptura sola* of the Reformation.
55. See, e.g., N. N. Sarna, "The Modern Study of the Bible in the Framework of Jewish Studies," *Proceedings of the Eighth World Congress of Jewish Studies, 1981* (Jerusalem, 1983), 1:19–27.
56. Joseph Kimhi, *Sefer ha-galui*, pp.1–2.
57. Proverbs was especially cultivated in the Mediterranean world. Of the almost seventy medieval Proverbs commentaries I here catalogued, only about half a dozen are Ashkenazic. See Frank Talmage, "Mi-kitvei R. Avigdor Kara ve-R. Menahem Shalem," *Hagut u-maaseh*, ed. Alfred Greenbaum and Alfred Ivry (Haifa, 1982), p. 50, n. 12.
58. In Abrahams, *Wills*, p. 82.
59. Judah Ibn Tibbon, "A Father's Admonition," in Abrahams, *Wills*, p. 82.
60. Jacob Anatoli, *Malmad ha-talmidim* (Lyck, 1866), p. [10].
61. Cf. the perspectives on Duran's biblicism in Isadore Twersky, "Religion and

Law," in S. D. Goitein, ed., *Religion in a Religious Age* (Cambridge, Mass., 1974), pp. 75–77.

62. See, in general, *ibid.*, pp. 69–82.

63. Cf. *Maaseh efod*, p. 15: "some have been so foolish as to say that the study of Scripture is worthless."

64. See Liebermann, "Hellenism," p. 109, n. 62. Rashi's alternative explanation of *higgayon* in *Ber.* 28a is "childish conversation" *(mi-sihat yeladim)*. One of the classic interpretations of the root *hgh* referring to superficial reading is that of Joseph Kimhi cited by his son David in the *Sefer ha-shorashim*, ed. J. H. R. Biesenthal and F. Lebrecht (Berlin, 1847), s.v. *hgh*, p. 77: "My father . . . wrote that it means stammering and muttering *(gimgum ve-zifzuf)*." Cf. Wieder, *Judean Scrolls*, pp. 219–20, n. 5. *Higgayon* is connected to the verb *mahgim* also, although in a different sense, in *Teshuvot ha-geonim*, ed. A. E. Harkavy (Berlin, 1887), no. 302, p. 144. See Breuer, "Keep," pp. 245–46.

65. This was echoed by Jacob Ibn Habib, *Ein Yaakov*, 5 vols. (Jerusalem, 1960/ 61), vol. 1, Ber., pp. 55a–b.

66. See Moses ben Nahman, *Perush ha-torah le-rabbenu Moshe ben Nahman*, ed. C. B. Chavel, 2 vols. (Jerusalem, 1958/9) 1:6. On this theory in general, see Gershom Scholem, *On the Kabbalah and Its Symbolism*, trans. Ralph Manheim (New York, 1969), pp. 37–38.

67. Duran, *Maaseh efod*, pp. 11–14, 20; Talmage, *Kitvei pulmos*, pp. 29; 65, n. 37; Ben Yehudah, *Millon*, 7:7265–66.

68. See my "Trauma at Tortosa: The Testimony of Abraham Rimoch." *Mediaeval Studies* 47 (1985) 384–385.

69. The presence of the family name, Kara, presumably related to *mikra* (Scripture) among Ashkenazim (Joseph Kara in France, Avigdor Kara in Bohemia) should be noted.

70. MS Zürich Zentralbibliothek Heid. 102, fol. 99v. The story was retold in Naphtali Bacharach, *Emek ha-melekh* (Amsterdam, 1647/8), p. 15a and in Simhah Assaf, "Iggerot mi-Zefat," *Kovez al yad* 13 (1939), p. 120. See Moshe Idel's and my forthcoming edition of the theological writings of Avigdor Kara.

71. See most recently Joseph Hacker, "R. Yosef Hayyun ve-dor ha-gerush mi-Portugal," *Zion* 48 (1982/3): 273–80.

72. Joseph Hayyun, *Millei de-avot* (Venice, 1595), p. 59b.

73. According to Breuer, "Keep," pp. 256–57, relates the negative Sephardic attitude toward Scripture in this period went hand in hand with hostility toward the study of secular sciences due to Ashkenazic influence in the Peninsula.

74. Meyer Kayserling, *História dos Judeus em Portugal*, trans. from the German ed. of 1867 by G. B. Corrêa da Silva and Anita Novinsky (Sao Paulo, 1971), pp. 64-65. At the time of writing, I did not have the opportunity to ascertain which of these commentaries might be extant.

75. Joseph Hacker, "Li-demutah ha-ruhanit shel Yehudei Sefarad be-sof ha-meah ha-hamesh esreh," *Sefunot* 2 (17) (1983): 54.

76. An apparent combination of rejection and acceptance can be found in the *Seder ha-yom* of Moses ibn Machir of Safed in the sixteenth century who advises that "the child's spending five years on Scripture is sufficient since it is a virtue which is not virtue. Its only purpose now is to fill the child's belly with the content and narratives of Scripture, Torah, Prophets, and Writings and to know how to read it with grammatical precision. But now is not the time for exegesis for when he studies gemara [after age fifteen], when he has much time, he can spend time in exegesis of Scripture" (Assaf, *Mekorot*, 3:19). This would have seemed to be the program of even an "anti-biblicist" like Hayyun who spent his later years on Scripture but in the context of rabbinics and theology.

Some Medieval Perceptions
of the Controversy
on Jewish Law

Edward A. Synan

I. THE ISSUE

Beneath the theme "medieval perceptions of the controversy on Jewish Law" lies another which remains a stone of stumbling to Jews on one hand and to Christians on the other. This is the notion of "supersession." A new covenant, it is alleged by Christians, has replaced the old covenant with the Jewish people.

There are reasons for thinking that this theme is of pressing importance for our time. Twice during the last few years it has been raised in the North American press; this could hardly have been anticipated. What, we may ask, lies beneath these resurrections?

Our earliest account of Christian religious practice indicates that the first members of the Church, all of Jewish background, continued to attend the Temple rites (Acts 3:1–26) and, as Peter's vision at Joppa shows (*ibid.* 10:9–16), to maintain Jewish dietary restrictions. Paul himself, Apostle to the Gentiles though he considered himself to be (Galatians 2:2), went first into the synagogue of each city he visited and that on the Sabbath (Acts 13:14, 17:2 etc.), nor did he neglect to circumcise Timothy who had been born of a Jewish mother and a Gentile father (*ibid.* 16:1–3).

Against all this, however, Peter reported an experience in which he was convinced that a divine revelation had assured him that no food ought to be considered "common," *mē koinou* (*ibid.* 10:15); Peter's ambiguous practice on the point provoked conflict between him and Paul (Galatians 2:11–14). Finally, the leaders of the Christian community in Jerusalem, Peter and Paul included, took counsel and reached the momentous decision that converts from paganism to the Church ought not to be bound by the full range of Jewish precepts.

Three episodes, therefore, the experience of Peter on the matter of diet, the opposition offered by Paul to Peter's "dissembling" in the face of pressure from Jewish converts to impose Jewish Law on Gentile converts, and the decision of the Jerusalem community leaders not to bind converts from the Gentile world to specifically Jewish practices, became the points of reference for future Christian speculation on the status of Jewish Law. This last episode, the decision of the Jerusalem Church, has been handed down in a notable letter for which Acts 15:23–29 is our source. So solemn an intervention might have been thought to settle the matter in a definitive way, at least insofar as Christians are concerned. For the language of Acts is formal: The decision not to hold converts from paganism to any Jewish precepts other than "those necessary ones," *toutōn tōn epanankes* (the avoidance of idol-offerings, of meat containing its blood or strangled things, and sexual license), was a solution with the force of divine revelation: it had "seemed good to the Holy Spirit and to us" (*ibid.* 15:28). Yet two eminent Christians have lately raised the issue anew, one directly, the other indirectly.

1. Karl Rahner on Christianity's Matrix

The first of these revivals, on an austerely theoretical plane, appeared appropriately enough in a theological journal. Professor Karl Rahner S.J. (whose death occurred between the first and the present drafts of this essay) received an honorary degree from the Weston School of Theology, Cambridge, Massachusetts, in April of 1979. *Theological Studies* published an English translation of his address to the Convocation on that occasion under the title: "Toward a Fundamental Theological Interpretation of Vatican II."[1]

Rahner there maintained that the initiative of the Jerusalem Church in ruling that Gentile converts not be held to Jewish legal prescriptions had set free the nascent Church from Hebrew bonds that would have blocked the evangelization of the Hellenistic world. In a bold tripartite periodization of Christian history, Professor Rahner asserted that before the events recorded in Acts 15, the Church was a Jewish reality (p. 721). From that decision until the Second Vatican Council, an asymmetrically long era in comparison with the first period, Christianity has been a European affair, an "export product" with respect to the great worlds of Asia, Africa, and the Americas (p. 717).

The opening of the Church to the Greek world at the price of a rupture with that of Judaism in its turn shackled what ought to be a world Church by binding it to European forms. If Rahner is right, twenty years ago the great Council inaugurated a third period of Christian history by shattering in principle a formidable obstacle to the evangelization of the worlds that lie beyond Europe and its appendages. This has been done through a new openness to the religions and to the cultures of the rest of our planet. Hellenism, in its latter-day European incarnation, has thus gone the way of Judaism as a limiting characteristic of the Church. Now, at long last, the Church is on the verge of becoming truly a "world religion" in fact as well as in aspiration. In short, to paraphrase Rahner's language, the Church is on the threshold of becoming authentically and fully "catholic" and this, thanks to a liberation from a cultural matrix comparable to the liberation of the apostolic Church from the matrix of Judaism.

Finally, Rahner was ready to concede that the "caesura" dividing Christianity from Judaism may have been unclear to Paul himself: "One need not think that he reflected with theological adequacy on this transition whose protagonist he was" (*ibid.* p. 727). Rahner insisted that it remains unclear to us:

[There are] theological problems involved in this transition from Jewish to Gentile Christianity, problems that are by no means so simple as people think, theologically difficult problems still to be worked out correctly; it is not yet reflectively clear to us what Paul "brought about" when he declared circumcision and everything connected with it superfluous for non-Jews (and perhaps only for them) . . . (*ibid.* p. 721).

2. Definition of a Jew

A second evocation of our theme, this time on a concrete plane, occurred in the secular press. The Paris bureau chief of *The New York Times,* John Vinoccur, produced a "cover story" article in the March 20, 1983 Sunday Magazine section of that paper on Cardinal Lustiger, Archbishop of Paris and, from his adolescence, a convert from Judaism.[2] Not everyone perceives in the same way the Cardinal's relationship to the Jewish people from among whom he springs. As he sees himself, the Cardinal has not ceased to be a Jew, despite his conversion to Christianity. In the view of some others, both Jews and Catholics, his claim is unintelligible. Still, not all their disclaimers proceed on the same basis.

Two rabbis, one a former Chief Rabbi of Paris, Meyer Jais, the other

Rabbi Michael Williams who presides at a synagogue in the rue Copernic (scene of an anti-semitic terrorist bombing in 1980), were quoted in the article as dissenting from the Cardinal. The first stated that a Jew who accepts Christianity "does not take up authentic Judaism, but turns his back to it" (*ibid.* p. 77).

Rabbi Williams made a more nuanced, but equally negative, comment:

> In any real terms, in emotional terms, in psychological terms, he is no longer a Jew. . . . Morally he is most certainly not, and yet he is obviously a sensitive, intelligent man, who, although a Christian, although someone who has left the Jewish world, has a great understanding and affection for it *(ibid.)*.

Nor is dissent on the conjunction of the Cardinal's baptism with his claim to be a Jew confined to Jewish observers. An Abbé Barbara was quoted in the same article as putting bluntly the dismay he feels: "What upsets me is someone who says, 'I'm a Jew and I intend to remain one.' The Apostles broke with the synagogue" *(ibid.)*.

The Cardinal himself produced an observation that was given special prominence by the editors who enclosed his statement in a frame and which expresses a kind of inversion of the Rahner thesis. "Look, friend, the West is born of Christianity, and the crisis of the West is that it isn't Christian anymore. Period" *(ibid.)*. For Cardinal Lustiger it is important that the Church determined our western culture; for Rahner, Hellenistic culture has determined the Church and that to her loss. Thanks to their diverse perspectives, these diverse appreciations are compossible and both positions have their values. In the terminology often used by medieval theologians, the positions are *diversa, non adversa,* "diverse, but not opposed."

These reservations, both Jewish and Catholic, are grounded upon a number of unspoken assumptions, not least of which is what "to be a Jew" may or must mean. The Cardinal's critics from the rabbinate undoubtedly have in mind the practice of the Jewish liturgy, the Sabbath above all, dietary observances, circumcision, and the denial, not only of divinity to Jesus of Nazareth, but also the denial of his claim to be Messiah. Abbé Barbara may well share all these convictions on what it is to be a Jew. For those Catholics who think with him (and his was surely the standard attitude in Catholic circles until very recent times), just as a Jew must say "no" to Jesus, so a Catholic must say "no" to the claim that a Jew can remain a Jew after baptism. Abbé Barbara gave his reason: "The Apostles broke with the synagogue." This is a particular exegesis of Acts 15:23–29. On his reading of the decision there recounted, the

Jerusalem Church legislated decisively and permanently that Church and Synagogue are in essential contradiction to each other. Such a reading, it must be remarked, has extrapolated the implications of that decision with a rigor unknown, for instance, to Paul who could write: "Are they Hebrews? So am I. Israelites? So am I. Abraham's descendants? So am I. Are they servants of Christ? I am mad to speak like this, *paraphronōn lalō,* but I can outdo them, *hyper egō*" (2 Corinthians 11: 22–23).

Rahner has posed many challenges that exceed our capacity to meet. It would require a self-confidence indistinguishable from arrogance to announce the final clarification of the issues raised in Rahner's address, above all, the enigmas that surround Paul's interventions and the decision of the Jerusalem Church to concede freedom from Jewish Law to converts from among the Gentiles:

> Today, as a matter of fact, perhaps even in contrast to patristic and medieval theology, we do not have a clear, reflective theology of this break, this new beginning of Christianity with Paul as its inaugurator; perhaps that will only gradually be worked out in a dialogue with the Synagogue of today (p. 723).

Yet such a clarification must be at the disposal of the theologian who purports to throw light on the essence of revelation, on a decisive ranking of theological truths in their hierarchy, on the details of what the Church ought to do with respect to the "great world religions":

> None of us can say exactly how, with what conceptuality, under what new aspects, the old message of Christianity must in the future be proclaimed in Asia, in Africa, in the regions of Islam, perhaps also in South America, if this message is really to be present everywhere in the world (p. 725).

Now, not to do everything is not identical with doing nothing. The modest first objective of these reflections is to call into council two medieval theologians in a way that, one hopes, will be neither patronizing nor uncritical, on how Rahner's "caesura" between the Jewish and the Gentile Church might be seen and appraised.

A further objective will be to invite that dialogue between Synagogue and Church in which Rahner suggested that solutions might be "worked out." This second step will include, with full realization that Church Order rests ultimately with the College of Bishops and in a particular way with the Bishop of Rome, the proposal of one response the Church might make to a crisis that clearly did not die with the decision of Acts 15.

II. GROSSETESTE

Robert Grosseteste, professor of theology at Oxford from about 1214 until 1235, and, from 1235 until his death in 1253, Bishop of Lincoln, has left three documents which testify to his interest in Jews and Judaism.[3] One of these is a letter to the Countess of Winchester who had asked for his expert opinion on her obligations with respect to Jews living within her jurisdiction, including the oversight of a *domus conversorum* on her estates for Jewish converts to Christianity. Second, Grosseteste wrote a commentary on the Epistle to the Galatians in which, it will be remembered, Paul recounted that he had opposed Peter "to his face," *kata prosōpon* (Galatians 2:11), on what Paul counted weakness under Jewish pressure to bend Gentile converts to the full range of Jewish Law. There is an allusion to this work (MS Bodleian lat. th. c. 17, fol. 167vb, 11. 37–45) in the third component of his Jewish dossier. This last is a full-scale theological tractate in two parts on the "cessation" of the legal precepts of Judaism, *De cessacione legalium*. What follows on Grosseteste is based on the first part of this work.

This section of his treatise is of interest here because in it Grosseteste came to grips with the crisis provoked in the Jerusalem Church by biblical texts which, literally interpreted, seemed to give eternal validity to all Jewish precepts. The second part is less pertinent here since in it he tried to establish that the messianic prophecies of the Hebrew Scriptures have been fulfilled in Jesus of Nazareth. It ought to be noted in passing that Grosseteste was celebrated for his command of Greek and that he seems to have had at least an elementary knowledge of Hebrew.

Scholars formerly thought that the conjunction of these three writings reveal a plan to convert Jews on the part of the Bishop of Lincoln. This interpretation has been abandoned since a landmark article by the lamented Professor Beryl Smalley who, like Professor Rahner, has died between versions of this paper. Her view is that in his work on Galatians and in the *De cessacione legalium* Grosseteste was primarily preoccupied with the historical-theological enigma rather than with a conversionist program.[4]

1. Positing the Question

In the first part of the *De cessacione*, Grosseteste proceeded in a thoroughly "scholastic" mode. His opening words set his problem in its historical context:

> There were many in the primitive Church who claimed that the rites, *sacramenta*, of the Old Law must be observed along with the rites of the New

Law for there is no salvation apart from their observance. Their opinion was condemned by the decree of the Apostles, written down in the Acts of those same Apostles, and it was most effectively refuted by the blessed Paul in epistles to the Romans and to the Galatians (ms. cit. fol. 158ra, 11. 1–6).

Having thus raised the issue Grosseteste was to adduce, in accordance with medieval university practice, strong reasons against the position he intended to defend and then to marshal the distinctions and principles that he felt would meet those arguments in opposition. He showed so acute a perception of what genuinely meeting an objection entails that his words merit citation in full:

. . . it is not appropriate to adduce assertions of the said Apostles and those of sacred exegetes, *expositorum,* since these objections are made by people who dispute against those very Apostles as well as against our Catholic exegetes and against all who abolish the ceremonial precepts. These latter cannot defend themselves with a mere assertion, or with an exegesis of texts from the Old Testament and the Gospel, an exegesis which they cannot make secure without irrefragable reasoning or an evident application of the Old Law or the Gospel. So it is that in this disputation we, playing the role, *gerentes personam,* of the Apostles and of the exegetes who abolish and destroy the ceremonial precepts, cannot bring in anything, as a response to those who want to prove the [necessity for the] observance of the ceremonial precepts, which we cannot show to be solid, whether by irrefragable reasoning or by an authoritative text of the Old Testament or of the Gospel (ms cit. fol. 159ra, 11. 7–21).

Every historian of medieval thought will recognize traces of a formal "disputed question" in Grosseteste's organization of his *De cessacione.* First, there is a statement of the question to be canvassed and we have seen him specify that not every Jewish precept is to be impugned. He has sharpened the focus to what he termed "ceremonial" precepts. Second, he was ready to give the opposition as strong a voice as his limited capacities might permit:

We shall set down some points which seem to confirm their opinion, to the degree that these occur to our small and impoverished talent and memory (ms cit. fol. 158ra, 11. 10–12).

Third, because no theologian could leave it at that, he promised to do what he could to refute those arguments he had raised in the name of his opponents:

These [arguments] having been set down in accord with our limitation, and dissolved in their proper places, we shall set down as well some points which disprove this error and which confirm the view that the Law has been rendered void through grace (ms cit. fol. 158ra, 11. 12–15).

2. Natural Law

His opening gambit in behalf of his own position was to establish the setting within which salvation history has unfolded and to correlate the broad divisions of that history with various forms of law. The most fundamental and universal of all laws is "natural law." This law ("alone" he will say) has characterized the period from Adam until Noah or, perhaps until Abraham (ms cit. fol. 162ra, 11. 39, 40), for both Patriarchs are associated with notable instances of "positive" law. Sacrifices and oblations in their earliest occurrences were not, as one might have thought, imposed by positive law (ms cit. 162ra, 11. 44–47); natural law itself requires that gratitude be expressed, and such is the function of sacrificial rites. Noah is associated with the prohibition directed against eating flesh with blood in it (Genesis 9:4–5), and Abraham with the rite of circumcision (Genesis 17:9–14; ms cit. fol. 162ra, 11. 40–43). With these positive laws Grosseteste saw the beginning of the "Old Testament" in succession to a primeval epoch of natural law only. Here he can hardly be credited with total clarity and this not only owing to his ambiguity on whether the Old Testament began with Noah or with Abraham. The command to abstain from the fruit of the tree "of the knowledge of good and evil" (Genesis 2:15–17) is proffered as an instance of law on "indifferent" matters, that is, on what is neither knowable as forbidden in itself, nor derived from principles that are known of themselves, his explicit conception of positive law (ms cit. fol. 160rb, 11. 5–13); yet this command pre-dated the rule of positive law if that began with Noah or with Abraham. We ought not leave his discussion of positive law without noting a special value he saw in that category of law:

The obedience by which one obeys a precept in indifferent matter, which has no ground in reason prescribing that it ought to be done, but only in the authority of the one who commands, is more humble than that by which one obeys a self-justifying precept (ms cit. fol. 160rb, 11. 46–49).

The Lord Robert was impressed by the unwritten character of natural law and he had a facile explanation for the later writing down in sacred Scripture of what had been "written in the heart" (Romans 2:15, 2 Corinthians 3:2–3).

Owing to sin, human memory has weakened as, indeed, all human physical vigor has declined in our fallen state; where our long-lived forebears had no difficulty in remembering all natural law and even the complexities of positive law (ms cit. fol. 160rb, 11. 18–33 and fol. 162ra, 11. b,19), we cannot manage without the written Testaments. This notion that intellectual capacity follows upon moral worth is a theme which Grosseteste developed elsewhere. In a play on words he was fond of repeating, understanding, the *aspectus mentis,* "glance of the mind," is proportioned to morality, the *affectus mentis,* "the mind's affection."[5] Thus he had given the "liberal arts" a moral as well as an intellectual justification. In any case, he could claim:

> Reliable history, *hystoria certa,* is not transferred to posterity except through writing. It was necessary that the life, *uita,* and the way of life, *conuersacio,* of that People, prophetic of our salvation, be set forth in authentic Scripture (ms. cit. fol. 164va, 11. 25–28).

With all his world, Grosseteste acknowledged that Adam is the father of our race in the order of nature. The fact of sin, however, extended the notion of human unity, not only for Adam, but also for the Devil who had tempted him and for Jesus who, as Messiah, reversed the progressive triumph of sin over the human race. Grosseteste put his insight in the form of four ways in which all our race is "one person." We are one person in Adam, thanks to the nature we have received from him; it is not too much to say that "all humans are in some way Adam." Because Adam was the first transgressor, birth from him subjects us all to the law of concupiscence; in this mode too we constitute one person with Adam. Beyond Adam as transgressor is the Devil; "all who are given to crime," especially "those who are sinners to the end, along with their head, the Devil," constitute a kind of single person. Grosseteste here remembered the Pauline conception of "mystical body" in which Jesus is the "head" and Christians his "members" (1 Corinthians 6:5; 12:12, 27; Ephesians 1:22; 4:25; 5:29; Colossians 1:18; 2:10, 19), for he promptly added the last mode in which a human multitude can be one person, this time "Messiah, along with his body, which is the Church" (ms cit. fol. 162vb, 11. 13–35).

The Lord Robert concluded this analysis with the claim that, for all these reasons, the "legal rites and positive mandates of the Old Law ought to have ceased" and he added one reason more: thus "the powerful kindness of the Liberator would be the more manifest and love on the part of the one set free might be the more ardent" (ms cit. fol. 164ra, 11. 7–10).

In his next line he impugned the good faith of the Synagogue:

The human race knows, and so does the Synagogue thanks to patriarchs and prophets, that they cannot enter the gate of paradise (nor can they be drawn out of the pit of sin) not through free choice, nor through natural law, nor written law, nor through sacrifices and legal victims (ms cit. fol. 164ra, 11. 10–14).

To a degree his harsh pronouncement on the good faith of the Synagogue (and of excessively naturalist philosophers of free choice and natural law as well) is balanced by his concession that the Christian claim of Incarnation is "a thing at maximum remove from human capacity to believe, *res maxime remota ab humana credulitate*" (ms cit. fol. 164rb, 11. 18–23). Of all truths, not one enjoys so little probability as this; easier to believe that a single person might be both lion and man than to believe that one Person is both God and man. Lions and humans, after all, have many aspects in common; divinity and humanity have nothing in which they share: *non communicant in aliquo eodem* (ms cit. fol. 164rb 11. 23–26).

3. Jewish Witness

In a more positive mode, we have seen that the Lord Robert counted the Jewish life-story and the Jewish way of life as prophetic for the whole human race. Medieval Christians had traditionally seen the dolorous history of the Jewish People as the history of "witnesses" to the mis-step of their fathers in rejecting Jesus. Grosseteste too accepted the notion of a witness-People, but he did so in his own fashion. Reflecting that what goes on within the privacy of a human person, a Jewish prophet, for instance, can only be known through sensation or through an account, he held that public testimony was required and, of course, had been provided. The People from among whom Jesus was to be born was chosen for this ministry and this ministry was best exercised through the Scriptures (ms cit. fol. 164va, 11. 14–25). Scripture, however, provides not only public testimony, but also intricate problems. The Hebrew Scriptures, for instance, often speak of the eternal character of circumcision, of the Sabbath, of dietary restrictions, and those Scriptures were held in honor by the Bishop of Lincoln. He had, therefore, to contrive a systematic theory of interpretation if he were to defend what he took to be the faith of the Christian Church on the issue of those "eternal" precepts, now, in Christian circles, not only thought to be "superfluous," but even to be mortally sinful. In so doing Grosseteste was not content simply to appeal to the exegetical tradition, already venerable in his day, of the "four senses" of Scripture, the historical-literal, the allegorical, the tropological-moral, and the anagogical. For his purposes two senses, the historical-literal and the allegorical, seemed adequate; as between these two, Grosseteste showed a common-sensical bias in favor of the literal sense that anticipated the view of Thomas Aquinas, for more than once he referred to the "obscurity" and "enigmatic" quality of allegorical interpretation. What he felt was wanted was a criterion on which one might recognize the necessity in some texts to move away from the more evident literal sense.

To this end Grosseteste distinguished four "parts" of Scripture. In one part the words signify the creatures of this world in their classes and through these they signify in a secondary way aspects of our redemption. A second part of Scripture signifies the "doings and the way of life of the People of Israel" and through such accounts signifies "what pertains to the salvation of the human race." His third part signifies what pertains to our salvation "in naked terms, that have nothing of enigmatic allegory," whereas a fourth part contains prophecy: "It is so contrived that whatever it may signify through allegory grounded in things, it also signifies the very same in naked words with no allegory" (ms cit. fol. 164va, 1. 52-b 9). At this point it seemed right to Grosseteste that he formulate his criterion for the interpretation of any and all scriptural passages:

> This, therefore, ought the student of the Scripture weigh: Wherever in this Scripture the first meaning of the words expresses our saving faith or charity, there no allegory is to be sought. Where the first meaning of the words signifies created things or the particular actions of a human way of life, there the realities, *res,* primarily signified through the words signify in a secondary way certain mysteries of our salvation (ms cit. fol. 164vb, 11. 10–17).

With this somewhat abstract criterion in place, the Lord Robert proceeded to show how it operates in practice. He chose for this a line of extreme obscurity from the Song of Songs: "Your teeth are like a flock of ewes just shorn . . . each ewe has twins" (Canticle 4:2). "Literally understood," he wrote with some justification, "this does not build up faith or charity." He went on, however, to clarify his criterion: "The realities, here signified by the words, signify some other matters that do pertain to faith or morals" (ms cit. fol. 164vb, 11. 41–47). As he noted a few lines farther, "this" (the twin progeny of the ewes) "has no suitable literal sense" (ms cit. fol. 164vb, 11. 53–55). His own, non-literal interpretation then was that "to bear twin progeny" means that one "love God and neighbor" (ms cit. fol. 165ra, 11. 7,8).

This did not exhaust his ingenuity. In the search for an acceptable meaning of any given passage, the rule enunciated ought to be reinforced by comparison of the verses at stake with other biblical passages in order to determine what an obscure line might mean for faith or for morals (ms cit. fol. 165 ra. 11. 44–46).

Since Grosseteste was a Christian convinced that Acts 15 had signaled the end of Jewish ceremonial precepts, the literal-historical meaning of texts in the Hebrew Scriptures concerning those ceremonial laws demanded just such comparison. Texts on the Sabbath, for instance, literally taken, make its observance perpetual, whereas others announce that it will end; if one applied his criterion "diligently" it would be seen that the author of Scripture

> . . . intended, not so much to signify through the name "Sabbath" the fact of corporeal rest, as to signify through that very corporeal fact a cessation from sin (ms cit. fol. 165ra, 11. 45–b 5).

Of the two exegetical options available on his principles, a holiday in the corporeal order, or abstinence from sin, Scripture and its Author wished principally to teach and even to command the second, moral, meaning and not the merely corporeal injunction (ms cit. 165rb, 11. 13, 14). Hence the Lord Robert wrote:

> In various passages of Scripture the Sabbath is "perpetual" and yet is "going to end," something that could not be the case with respect to what is one and the same. What is more evident than that, when the Sabbath is said to be "perpetual," this ought to be understood of the moral Sabbath, the literal Sabbath understood as "going to end"? (ms cit. fol. 165rb, 11. 36–40).

It would be tedious to follow Grosseteste through his systematic application of his criterion to circumcision and to the prohibition against eating flesh in which the blood is still present. Perhaps it will suffice to note that, as the Sabbath became, in his view, not abstinence from labor so much as abstinence from sin, thus circumcision became the fleshly sign of taking what is superfluous "from the heart," with, of course, appeal to Jeremiah 4:4 and 9:26 (ms cit. fol. 165va, 11. 19–34). Even the precept against eating meat containing blood, one of the exceptions permitted by Acts 15 as "necessary," he thought less than necessary and a literal reading of Leviticus 17:11, "The life of a creature is in the blood," a "frivolous" exegesis. "Life," he pointed out, "is in the flesh as well" (ms cit. fol. 166ra, 11. 2–12). As for the complicating factor that the Jerusalem Church had left this precept in place, Grosseteste appealed to the time-honored cliché of the "hardness of Jewish hearts" to explain why it was not precisely "forbidden," but that the observance of the precept was "permitted"; else the Jewish Christians would have been "excessively scandalized" (ms cit. fol. 166ra, 11. 23–28).

Finally, the Lord Robert noted that "testimony precisely as testimony" and a "sign precisely as a sign" argue the absence, even the privation, of that to which testimony is given, that which a sign signifies. The Hebrew People and their Scriptures were, in his understanding, signs and witnesses of Messiah to come. "Hence, a sign, inasmuch as it is a sign, ceases when the manifest presence of the reality signified is manifested" (ms cit. fol. 166ra, 11. 58,59).

Grosseteste confided to his readers that there are many other effective arguments "some of which" he had written down when expounding Galatians, at least insofar as he could, and so he felt free to move to the authorities of both the Old and the New Law as well as to the unanimous consent of Christian exegetes who had set out the truth of the matter (ms cit. fol. 167vb, 11. 41–45).

Since it is inappropriate to delay over his scriptural dossier, only two points will be noted. The line of Ezekiel 20:25, "I imposed on them statutes that were not good statutes and laws by which they could not win life," beloved of Christian controversialists in this material, Grosseteste simply cited without comment. A second point worthy of mention is that, unlike the majority of medieval Christian theologians, Grosseteste here expressed no preference between the positions of Augustine and of Jerome on the moment when the Jewish Law ceased to bind, when the Gospel had been widely disseminated or at the moment of Jesus' death; he was content to present the two views with no comment.

III. AQUINAS

In certain aspects the texts which Thomas Aquinas contributed to our theme are parallel to those of Robert Grosseteste. Both theologians responded to noble ladies' questions on their duties as feudal rulers of vassals whose number included Jews with the special problems posed by Jewish money-lending at interest for those who received rents from them, Grosseteste to the Countess of Winchester, Aquinas to the Countess of Flanders (not, as often claimed, to the Duchess of Brabant). Like Grosseteste, Brother Thomas produced an exegetical study of Galatians (and one on Romans as well); finally, on occasions both early and late in his career, Aquinas dealt with the problem of the legal precepts in an even more formal scholastic mode than had the Bishop of Lincoln. The first of these was his *Scriptum super libros Sententiarum,* his *Writing on the Books of Sentences* (of Peter Lombard) and the second, his *Summa theologiae*, the great *Summary of Theology*.

Not only on the plane of literary genre, but also on that of theological reasoning, Aquinas carried forward traditions exemplified by Grosseteste. As Beryl Smalley remarked, Aquinas "put forward a theoretical justification for the wider meaning now currently accorded to the literal sense, and distinguished it from the spiritual senses more clearly than had been done before."[6] By defining the literal sense as "all that the human writer intended" Aquinas "cleared up a persistent muddle in terminology" (p. 54) and by his distinction "made firmer ground for the rule (already partly accepted) that argument must proceed from the literal sense only" (pp. 54–55). Last, she characterized Brother Thomas, correctly in my view, as "an intelligent conservative. He thought out the traditional doctrine and put his learning at its disposal" (p. 67).

1. Views on Jews and Judaism

In Jewish-Catholic dialogue it must be noted that Aquinas in no sense anticipated the ecumenical goals that motivate us. True enough, he more than once defended the right of Jewish parents to determine the education of their children in Judaism and condemned the efforts by Christian zealots to take and to baptize such children.[7] Still, this inhibition, based upon his conviction that natural law concedes to parents the right to make the choices their infant children cannot make for themselves, hardly extends to a renunciation of conversionist missions by Christian to Jews and still less to the concession that "ceremonial" law might retain some value in the Christian era. Two "saint's lives" written to forward his canonization recount his having conferred with two "learned and wealthy Jews" and that both of them accepted baptism after hearing his responses to their inquiries.[8]

Furthermore, although without any doubt a most expert interpreter of sacred Scripture on the standards of his time, Aquinas (unlike Grosseteste) knew no biblical language, nor was the form in which the Latin Vulgate Bible circulated in the Paris of his day a text such as modern scholarship would esteem. His strongest suit was the orderly and metaphysically penetrating understanding of texts, not the sympathetic grasp of the atmosphere of the Jewish world which had produced the Scriptures, the New Testament as well as the Old. The Jewish world was reduced in his time to tiny clusters of Jews in alienated and alien communities, separated, partly by their own choice and partly by harsh legislation which popular prejudice reinforced, from the mainstream of Christian life around them.

2. Understanding of Apostolic Writings

A few instances will clarify these disabilities on the part of so able a theologian. The epistles of Paul, so germane to the issue, are classic examples of "occasional" writing. An emergency here (Philemon 8–16), a scandal there (2 Timothy 4:14), a report from Corinth (1 Corinthians 7:1ff.), personal friends in Thessalonica (1 Thessalonians 1:6–10), would move the Apostle to write letters which are a world removed from the stylized and metaphysical writing of thirteenth century university masters; yet Aquinas imposed upon this corpus a scholastic grid. Thus the First Epistle to the Corinthians, he announced, deals with "sacraments," whereas the second epistle to the same Church deals with "the ministers" of those sacraments. After these two epistles, thus given status as theological tractates, there "necessarily follows the Epistle to the Galatians in which the theme is the cessation of Old Testament rites."[9] In Galatians, Aquinas explained, Paul "made use of syllogism in the second figure," that is, of a syllogism in which the middle term holds the predicate place in both premises (*ibid.* cap. 3, lect. 4, ed. cit. p. 597, # 140). His conception of the truth of sacred Scripture is absolute; explanations, therefore, that square better with the very words of Paul are "truer" on that account (*ibid.* cap. 2, lect. 3, p. 584, # 88). The traditional Aristotelian distinction between "formal" and "final" causality seemed to him useful in understanding how the "works of the virtues" can be the objects of our seeking; they are to be sought "for their own sake formally, but not finally," that is, as precisely determined means, but for a goal beyond themselves (*ibid.* cap. 5, lect. 6, p. 636, # 328).

Even more serious was the persuasion of Aquinas that there was hostility on the part of Jews against Christians, from the beginning up until his own time. "Jews had persecuted Paul," he wrote, "precisely because he taught that the legal rites ought not to be observed" (*ibid.* cap. 5, lect. 2, p. 629, # 295) and he supported this interpretation with a short detour through Roman history. The Roman Emperors had granted Jews the right to observe their ceremonies in peace, whereas Christianity was proscribed by imperial decrees. This led to a double peril for Christians: "Whoever believed in Christ, but was not circumcised, became vulnerable to persecution, whether by the Gentiles or by the Jews" (*ibid.* cap. 6, lect. 3, p. 646, # 368), by the Romans because a Christian lacked the Jewish legal immunities and by the Jews because a Christian lacked the sign of Jewish solidarity. What was more, he was convinced, "This they [the Jews] would do now, if they could," *et facerent etiam nunc si possent* (*ibid.* cap. 4, lect. 9, p. 624, # 272).

Brother Thomas opened his *lectura,* his "lecturing," on Galatians with a blanket statement of that epistle's nature, a statement that can be matched in Grosseteste (ms cit. fol. 189ra, 11. 38–44): in it, as Aquinas read his epistle, Paul "rebuked the Galatians who had been so far seduced by a fraudulent teacher that they would keep simultaneously the legal precepts and the Gospel" (*In ad Galatas*, prologus ed. cit. p. 563, # 1).

Another *crux exegetica* which exercised Brother Thomas and which tells us something about his equipment to meet the challenge of New Testament problems is the variation in Paul's practice with respect to the circumcision of Timothy and that of Titus. According to Aquinas:

> The particular reason why Timothy was circumcised and Titus not was that Timothy was born of a Gentile father and a Jewish mother, whereas both parents of Titus were Gentiles. The decision of the Apostle was that those born of a Jewish parent on either side ought to be circumcised, but on no account ought those born entirely of Gentile parents be circumcised (ibid. cap. 2, lect. 1, p. 579, # 63).

Aquinas seems not to have taken in any rigid sense the sequence of events he found in Acts because Paul's refusal to submit Titus to the Law, narrated in Galatians 2:3, seemed to Aquinas the ground for the decision of the whole Jerusalem Church narrated in Acts 15:

> Whence [that is, from the case of Titus] was given that decision by the apostles on the compulsory non-observance of the legal precepts as is had in Acts xv [:28] (*ibid.* cap. 2, lect. 1, p. 579, # 61).

3. Ignorance of Law

Like Grosseteste, Aquinas was severe in his judgment of the sincerity of Jews contemporary with Paul. Of all moral norms, Aquinas put conscience in the first place and counted ignorance an excuse for erroneous, but conscientious, decisions. Ignorance, however, could not be pleaded in behalf of Jews who failed to acknowledge Jesus as Messiah; this, he held, was "ignorance of law" and such ignorance does not excuse because it is corrigible (*ibid.* cap. 5, lect. 1, p. 626, # 282). He went even farther in this direction by condemning the Jewish leadership for "affected ignorance," that is, an ignorance that took its origin from an attitude of wishing not to know the truth. Those Jewish *principes*, "principal men," knew that Jesus was Messiah because in him they had seen "all the signs . . . which the prophets had said would come to pass" (*Summa theologiae* 3.47.6, in corp.); their ignorance bore only on his divinity and it was this ignorance that "did not excuse them from crime because it was affected ignorance" (*Summa theologiae* 3.47.5, in corp.).

In the same question of his *Summa* Aquinas calibrated three levels of "ignorance" with three corresponding levels of guilt with respect to the rejection and execution of Jesus. The first and heaviest guilt fell upon the "greater" among the Jews; their "sin was the greatest, both owing to its type and to wilful malice." A second level of guilt, that of the "lesser" among the Jews, was extremely grave owing to its type, but in "some degree lessened owing to their ignorance." Least of all was the sin of the Gentiles "through whose hands he was crucified, men who had no knowledge of the Law" (*Summa* 3.47.6, in corp.). The intimation that a knowledge of Jewish Law counts as an advantage in the sphere of faith (although somewhat paradoxical in its effect here) is not misplaced. Like all Christians, Aquinas made the epoch of the Hebrew Scriptures fundamental to his own Christian period; as is often mentioned in Jewish-Christian dialogue, Judaism has no need of Christianity, but Christianity needs Judaism. Besides, despite all these negative attitudes towards Judaism and the Jews must be noted the esteem Aquinas expressed for his Jewish fathers in faith:

It must, therefore, be stated, thanks to the special worship offered by them to God, He was God of the Jews alone, whence in Psalm 75(76): 1, it is said: "In Judah God is known; His Name is great in Israel." Still, He was God of all through His ruling of all things in common, according to the saying of Psalm 46(47): 7: "God is King of all the earth" (*In ad Galatas* cap 3, lect. 4, p. 56, # 319).

4. Sin and Salvation

On Paul's "Are they Hebrews? So am I . . ." Aquinas wrote: "This is a great compliment because, as is said, 'Salvation is of the Jews' " (John 4:22; *ibid*.). Should one reverse the import of Paul's remark that "We ourselves are Jews by birth, not Gentiles and sinners" (Galatians 2:15) by inferring that, therefore, the Jews are sinners, since that same John had written: "If we say that we have no sin, we deceive ourselves" (1 John 1:8), Aquinas was ready to apply a philosophical distinction to ease the tension. A single act may well be a sin, but only an ingrained habit justifies the term "sinner": "I answer that it is one thing 'to sin' and another 'to be a sinner,' for the first names one act, but the second a habit, a readiness toward sinning" (*In ad Galatas* cap. 2, lect. 4, p. 585, # 91).

What did Thomas Aquinas make of Paul's pronouncement that there is no distinction to be made in the Church between Jew and Gentile (Galatians 3:28)? This, for Aquinas, holds only with respect to gaining the goal which is salvation; meanwhile, he echoed Paul's assertion of a priority in favor of the Jews: "But with respect to the order of salvation, the Jews are first because to them were the promises made and into their grace were Gentiles taken, as if it were a branch of wild olive into a sound olive tree (see Romans 11:24); from them too was our Savior born" (*In ad Romanos* cap. 1, lect. 6, ed. cit. p. 20, # 101). Even the rites of the Jews, so often condemned by Christian critics (and this not only in the Middle Ages) as grossly material and all but pagan, were defended by Aquinas. He justified them with a distinction and a noetic parallel: pagans served and even worshiped the elements of this world, whereas Jews served and worshiped God under those elements, an order not only suitable, but even necessary as he saw it "because it is in harmony with human nature, which is led from sensible to intelligible things" (*In ad Galatas* cap. 4, lect. 1, p. 610, # 198).

5. Jewish Precepts

We have seen that Robert Grosseteste was content to distinguish two classes of Jewish precepts, the "moral" and the "ceremonial." Aquinas added a third, the "judicial," but the first two dominate his discussion. "Judicial" precepts he conceived to be those norms that regulate relationships between humans, not relationships between the human race and the Lord (*Summa* 1–2.99.4, in corp. and *Summa* 1–2.104, 1, in corp.). It is not without interest to know in our context that he thought these judicial precepts had "died" with the advent of Jesus, but that they need not be counted "death-dealing," that is, mortally sinful if observed after the advent of Jesus:

> If some prince should ordain in his kingdom that those judicial precepts be observed, he would not sin unless, perchance, they were observed in such a way (or commanded to be observed in such a way) as to imply that their obligatory force derived from an enactment of the Old Law (*Summa* 1–2.104.3, in corp.).

Hence, one may suppose, should the present-day State of Israel, for example, think it right to reinstate Old Testament legislation of this description on the purely civil plane and in a fully secular spirit, no objection could be made to this in the name of Thomas Aquinas. We shall see again his sensitivity to the implications of what one does or says; here, due cautions in place, unacceptable implications do not necessarily follow.

As for the "moral" precepts, like Grosseteste, and the whole Christian tradition on the matter, Aquinas counted them as permanent precisely because they coincide with natural law prescriptions (*Summa* 1–2.100.1, in corp.). For him, as is well known, "natural law" is the specifically human participation in "eternal law," in the rational intentions of the Creator which are revealed to us naturally in our authentically "natural" inclinations (*ibid.* 1–2.91.1 and 2). Both "moral" and "ceremonial" precepts Aquinas considered integral to, but not constitutive of, justification. The moral precepts clearly belong to natural human development, but so too do the ceremonial precepts insofar as their observance is a recognition of the divine (*Summa* 1–2.102.1 ad 3m and 102.3, in corp.) Aquinas sided with the opinion of Augustine as against that of Jerome on the moment at which the Old Law had ceased to bind; for Jerome this was the passion of Jesus (*Epistola* 112; PL 22 921–924) but for Augustine the time was vaguely indicated as when the Gospel had been promulgated (*Epistola* 82; PL 33 282–283). Despite their differences on the time, both Church Fathers held that the ceremonial precepts became "death-dealing" in the season of the grace of Christ and on this Aquinas followed their lead (*In ad Galatas* cap. 2, lect. 3, p. 583, # 86).

Because the *Summa theologiae* was echeloned over the last nine years of the saint's life, and remained unfinished at his death, its handling of our theme may be taken without reservation as his mature thought on the cessation of the ceremonial precepts. That the enigma of laws, announced by Holy Scripture to be both permanent and passing, preoccupied him to the end is visible in the extreme length of the *Summa* articles on the issue. To see this in objective terms, *Summa* 1–2.102.3, for instance, runs to more than nine columns in the Ottawa edition, the next article, 1–2.102.4, runs to more than fourteen, the next, 1–2.102.5 to more than eighteen and the next, 1–2.102.6 to more than eleven; this in an edition in which three columns sufficed for the celebrated "five ways" to demonstrate that the Holy One is, and must be. Examination of our theme at such unwonted length reflects his scrupulous concern to clarify, insofar as he could, every aspect of this puzzling problem. In the end, Aquinas reached a most negative conclusion on Jewish ceremonial Law. To observe those precepts after the advent of Jesus Messiah (an era calculated in Augustine's mode) was adjudged to be mortally sinful. As always, his reasoning is formidable:

> All ceremonies are a kind of witnessing-forth of faith. So it is that one can witness-forth an interior faith either by actions or by words and, in both cases, should one witness-forth anything false, one sins mortally. . . . The ancient fathers . . . preceded Christ, whereas we follow him. . . . What was

said by them, "A virgin will conceive and will bear a child" (Isaiah 7:14), words in the future tense, we represent through words in the past tense. . . . In a similar way, the ceremonies of the Old Law signified Messiah as "to be born" and as "to suffer in the future," whereas our sacraments signify that he "has been born," that he "has suffered" (*Summa* 1–2.103.4, in corp.).

Here, finally, is the nub of the Thomist solution: Ceremonies convey convictions and between "will be" and "has been" there can be no middle ground. His conscience as a believing Christian compelled him to say that Messiah "has been born," "has suffered." His conscience would not permit him to defend the persistence of rites which, as he saw them, look forward to a Messiah "yet to be born," "yet to suffer." Those rites, the Jewish "ceremonial Laws," seemed to be in irreducible opposition to his Christian faith.

IV. NEW BEGINNINGS

With this we reach the end of our examination of these two medieval theologians on the "cessation of the legal precepts." Both Robert Grosseteste and Thomas Aquinas followed the time-honored objective of deploying their resources in order to penetrate the meaning of what they believed, the Augustinian enterprise of faith examined with reverence and ingenuity in the hope of grasping to some degree its inner necessities. Neither one underestimated the difficulty of interpreting Scripture and neither one was enamored of the often fanciful "spiritual senses" that offer facile solutions. Grosseteste would allow a departure from the literal sense if and only if his rule could be applied and Aquinas would allow a theological argument to proceed from the literal sense only:

In Holy Scripture no confusion results for all the senses are founded on one sense, the literal, from which alone an argument can be drawn, not from those intended allegorically. . . . Nothing necessary to faith is contained under a spiritual sense which is not elsewhere put forward clearly by Scripture in its literal sense (*Summa* 1.1.10 ad 1m).

Neither theologian was conscious of a need to establish the faith-credentials of their conviction that Acts 15 announced the end of Hebrew ceremonial and that the most categoric prescriptions of the Hebrew Scriptures on those laws can be explained (not precisely "explained away") but brought into harmony with what they saw as the Christian completion of the Old Testament in a manner both respectful and intelligible.

Their academic tools for penetrating the meaning of the Bible are not the tools of modern scholarship, of course, but to respect the men and the work they were able to do with such equipment does not commit us to staying with their conclusions. It would be as little appropriate to adopt Thomistic exegesis as to arm our police and soldiers with the swords and armor of the knights who were the brothers of Aquinas. Our time challenges us to enter once more the lists in which the ceremonials of the Hebrew Law are at stake.

If anything can be retained from our medieval forebears it is their respect for faith as they struggled to perceive its implications. For us, the Cardinal of Paris can serve as archetype for what may well be a considerable number of Christians who count themselves Jews, despite their acceptance of Jesus as Messiah. This conviction, however numerous or few its partisans, demands our best efforts to consider in a serious and even radical way how it ought to be evaluated by Jews and by Christians. For Christians, as Rahner pointed out, a new ecclesial situation has opened doors long shut; to whom more than to Jews and to Jewish Christians ought the Church to be thus open? Aquinas was surely correct to claim that ceremonies practiced have consequences for faith, manifest faith, and he was not wrong to emphasize the tense in which we speak of what ''has been'' and of what ''will be.'' Is it necessary to stop where he stopped?

Advent Peoples

My suggestion is that Christians see in Jews and in Jewish Christians the ''witness People'' of Robert Grosseteste and that the Thomist disquiet over ''past'' and ''future'' be met by invoking Catholic Advent liturgy as a model. No Christian is conscious of denying faith in Jesus while developing during those weeks of preparation the anticipatory stance of Isaiah, of John the Baptist, of Mary. True enough, Jews are not unanimous on Messiah, but is it possible to be a Jew in any sense, yet not to long for the Kingdom? Can we Christians not see in those Jews who remain within Judaism an ''Advent People'' in one mode and in those Jews who have accepted Christianity an ''Advent People'' in another modality?

Many years ago a great man who was also a good friend, Abbot Leo Rudloff O.S.B., spoke to a Jewish-Christian gathering and made the point that the Christian Churches have been impoverished successively by the divisions that have arisen during their long histories. The most recent of these is the division of Western Christendom by the sixteenth century Reform and Counter-Reform. This followed upon the division many centuries before of Christianity into Eastern and Western Churches. Both these internal breaks followed on one even more disastrous, the division of the Church from the Synagogue, a division of which, it has been thought so long, the decision of Acts 15 was the occasion and the seal.

As for the forms that ought to be adopted in healing that first and worst of wounds, friendly encounters between Jews and Christians alone proffer hope of success. Neither Jewish nor Christian sensibilities can be offended, neither the Jewish nor the Christian conscience rowelled. Florence Nightingale once said (so the story goes) that ''whatever else hospitals do, they must not spread disease.'' Whatever else we may do, we must not spread more dissent, more bitterness, more misunderstanding. No merely institutional construct, a Jewish-Christian rite within the Christian Church, for instance, offers true hope. Apart from the air of artifice that poisons such adventures, we are sobered by the resentments in Christian Orthodox circles over Eastern Churches in communion with Rome.

Reluctant though a Christian must be to ''speak for'' Jews on how they ''ought'' to feel, we dare hope that Jews would not take umbrage at the image proposed of an Advent People as they wait with us for the mysterious working out in His time and in His way of our common fulfillment. We humans are responsive to images, to the words in which they are expressed, to the conceptual resources by which we attempt the penetration of an image or a word. Should Christians look upon Jews and Jewish Christians as two sorts of Advent People, Christian faith would be no more compromised than it is by our liturgical prayers and hopes during the Advent season opening each Church year.

Last, as no Catholic can speak for Jews, so one Catholic cannot speak for all Christians, nor even for all Catholics. The intention of these pages is no more than to invite each reader to think and speak and pray in the sure hope that the Lord we all worship will grant us His peace.

NOTES

1. *Theological Studies* 40.4 (1979) 716–727, translated by Leo J. O'Donovan S.J. A second English translation is to be found in *Theological Investigations* 20, a publication which regularly provides English versions of Rahner's writings.

2. *The New York Times Magazine,* November 20, 1983, ''A Most Special Cardinal''; this article is a model for bridging Jewish-Catholic traditions on a sensitive issue, here the unusual one of conversion followed by high ecclesiastical office.

3. The three documents are Grosseteste's *Epistola* 5, ed. H.R. Luard, Rolls Series (London: 1861), 33–38; *Commentarius in epistolam Pauli ad Galathas,* Oxford MS Magdalene 57, foll. 1a–32b; *De cessacione legalium,* Oxford MS Bodleian lat. th. c. 17; a critical edition of this work had been announced for the spring of 1984, but is

not yet available. An unpublished doctoral dissertation by Arthur M. Lee, University of Colorado, 1942, provides a transcription from MSS known to be extant at that date; since the Bodleian MS (which came into the possession of the Bodleian in 1948) has been corrected in Grosseteste's hand, Lee's readings have been controlled against a film of that MS.

4. Beryl Smalley, "The Biblical Scholar," in *Robert Grosseteste. Scholar and Bishop,* ed. D.A. Callus O.P. (Oxford: Clarendon Press, 1955), 70–97.

5. See for instance his *De finitate motus et temporis,* ed. L. Bauer, "Die Philosophischen Werke des Robert Grosseteste, Bischofs von Lincoln," *Beiträge zur Geschichte der Philosophie des Mittelalters,* Bd. 9 (Münster i. W., 1912), 105, 30–35 and his commentary on the *Posterior Analytics* of Aristotle, 1, 14 (81a 38–b 9) (Venice: 1514), fol. 17rb.

6. Beryl Smalley, "William of Auvergne, John of La Rochelle and St. Thomas Aquinas on the Old Law," in *St. Thomas Aquinas 1274–1974. Commemorative Studies,* ed. A.A. Maurer *et al.* (Toronto: Pontifical Institute of Mediaeval Studies, 1974), II, 11–71; the remark cited occurs on page 52.

7. The locus classicus is *Summa theologiae* II–II.10.12; the same position is taken in *Quodlibet* II, 4.2; the first of these works cited hereafter in the "Piana edition" (Ottawa: Commissio Piana, 1953) and the second in the "Marietti edition," *S. Thomae Aquinatis quaestiones quodlibetales,* ed. R. Spiazzi O.P. (Turin: Marietti, 1956).

8. Bernard Gui, "Life of St. Thomas Aquinas", in *The Life of St. Thomas Aquinas. Biographical Documents,* Kenelm Foster O.P., transl. and ed., XIV, 36; for the Latin text, cf. "Fontes vitae sancti Thomae Aquinatis," D. Pruemmer O.P., ed., in *Revue thomiste* (Toulouse 1911 and 1934), 96, 97, 181, 182.

9. *S. Thomae Aquinatis . . . super epistolas s. Pauli lectura,* R. Cai O.P., ed. (Turin: Marietti, 1953), in *Ad Galatas,* cap. 1, lect. 1, 565 # 2.

A Jewish Reading of St. Thomas Aquinas on the Old Law

Michael Wyschogrod

The relationship of Christianity to the Mosaic law has been a topic of intense debate from the very beginning of the new faith. It is dealt with at length in the Epistles of Paul and is not absent from the Gospels. Because of the prominence of the problem in these foundational documents, it remains a recurring topic in much subsequent Christian literature. And yet, it is not possible to assert that a satisfactory level of clarity has been achieved with respect to this question. In a recent study of one aspect of the problem—Paul's relationship to the law—E.P. Sanders comments that "the subject is difficult and all the scholarly labor that has been spent on it has resulted in no consensus."[1] It is probable that the same could be said about references to the law in the Gospels. While the passages there dealing with Jesus' attitude to the law are perhaps less convoluted than the writings of Paul, the Gospels nevertheless do not present an easily understandable teaching about the Mosaic law. We need only think of such apparent contradictions as that between Mt. 15:11 and 5:17–20 to be reminded of the difficulties. The problem of the law permeates the New Testament, even if it is most acute in the writings of Paul.

While the problem is an old one, its discussion in the context of Jewish-Christian diologue is new. When Thomas Aquinas dealt with this question (*Summa Theologiae,* 1a2ae, 98–108), he probably did not pay very much attention to how Jews would react to his treatment. He lived and wrote in a Christian world that was certain of the validity of its world-view and of the superiority of the new over the old covenant. While Thomas, particularly in the portion of the *Summa* referred to above, frequently cites Maimonides, one

125

does not get the feeling that the Judaism Maimonides represents is much of a challenge to Thomas. He is fully aware of the Old Testament roots of Christianity and of the necessity to take the law of the Old Testament seriously. It is therefore necessary to think through the question of the relationship of Christianity to the Old Law, and this is a task he performs with surprising attention to the details of the Old Law. The number of pages he devotes to the problem of the Old Law (over 150 in the Blackfriars edition) may signal a greater turbulence than appears on the surface. In any case, the time may have come for a Jewish reading of Thomas' treatment of the Old Law. While such a reading cannot be entirely non-polemical, it must attempt to grasp Thomas' truth from within his frame of reference, as far as that is possible for a Jewish reader.

DIVISIONS OF THE OLD LAW

Thomas does not specifically define the term "Old Law" but it is not difficult to fathom what he means by it: the Mosaic law. This emerges from Article 6 of Question 98 which inquires "whether it was appropriate that the Old Law should have been given at the time of Moses," a question which is answered affirmatively. By the Old Law Thomas means the legal portions of the Pentateuch. More interesting, however, is Article 2 of Question 98: "Whether the Old Law came from God," a question which is also answered affirmatively. But why would anyone have thought otherwise? Is it not axiomatic for Christians that the Old as well as the New Testament is divinely inspired and that the commandments which the Pentateuch ascribes to God are not human inventions? Thomas gives several reasons for holding the view that the Old Law did not come from God: it is imperfect, it did not last forever and it did not suffice for the salvation of man. If such a law can still be ascribed to God, it is only because, while the Old Law is abolutely imperfect, it was nevertheless perfect "for the purposes of some particular time" (Article 98, Reply 1). Since such relative perfection is the maximum perfection possible at a given time, it is worthy of God. The Marcionite position is apparently alive enough in the Church that it must be refuted.

Having established the divine origin of the Mosaic or Old Law, Thomas proceeds in Question 99 to divide the precepts of this Law into the moral, the ceremonial and the judicial. Such a division is not, in itself, surprising. Thomas follows here, as in so many other places, the Aristotelian conviction that classification is the key to understanding. Thomas knows very well that the Old Law is not going to prove permanent, that there will come a time, or a time has come, when the Old Law, or at least a portion of it, will have been abolished. If this is to be made intelligible, the Old Law must be divided into sharply defined categories so that one segment of it can be considered no longer binding while another can remain in full force. The other alternative is to declare the whole of the Old Law no longer in effect, but that is not very plausible in view of the positive statements about the Mosaic law in the New Testament. But because of the negative statements about the law in the New Testament, a portion of it must end with the coming of Jesus. In the light of the need to distinguish the permanent from the transient in the Old Law, making the proper distinctions within the Old Law becomes a matter of central importance.

One segment of the Old Law consists of the moral law. The moral law, in turn, is coextensive with the natural law (100,1). About the natural law, Thomas writes (94,3,Reply. All quotations are from the Blackfriars edition):

> All things have a natural tendency toward activity befitting their natures, like fire to heating. Since the rational soul is man's proper form, he has a natural tendency to act according to reason, that is to say according to virtue. Consequently in this sense all acts of virtue are of natural law, for each man's own reason naturally dictates that he should act virtuously.

Examples of the natural law in the Old Testament are "Honor thy father and thy mother," "Thou shalt not murder," and "Thou shalt not steal" (100,1,Reply). It follows that with respect to the part of the Old Law that is the natural law, revelation was not really necessary, at least in theory. In practice, the reason of man is not perfect and there is therefore no harm in including the natural law in the revelation of the Old Testament since without such revelation the natural law would be known only by the elite of humanity and perhaps even by it not perfectly. The main point is that the moral portion of the Old Law is the natural law known by all rational humanity.

In addition to the moral precepts, the Old Law also contains ceremonial precepts. They are "those precepts of the Law which are concerned with the worship of God . . ." (99,3, Reply). Thomas understands that the ceremonial precepts cannot be distinguished too sharply from the natural law since in man's relationship with God certain principles of the natural law such as the obligation to be grateful for favors done come into play. Nevertheless, the principles of the natural law are general and there is a need to apply these principles in concrete situations. Such application with respect to the worship of God constitutes the revealed ceremonial law. Because a similar application to concrete cases is also required for those aspects of the natural law that deal with human relations, Thomas maintains that "the concrete application of the universal principles that justice must be observed among men is made by means of judicial precepts" (99,4, Reply). The judicial precepts derive their fundamental justification from the natural law, but because they are the application of the natural law to concrete cases, they derive their force not from reason alone but from enactment. And the same is true of the ceremonial law which derives its force from the enactment of regulations dealing with the worship of God.

In short, the Old Law has three parts. One is the moral law which corresponds to the natural law and the other two are the ceremonial and judicial precepts which deal with the applications of the universal principles of the natural law to the worship of God and to human relations respectively. The ceremonial and judicial precepts derive their force from divine enactment and could not be deduced from the natural law alone. Thomas' argument can be understood if we apply his reasoning to the traffic laws. The natural law dictates that human life be safeguarded but it does not dictate that drivers must stay on the right side of the road or that a particular street be one-way. These specific regulations must be enacted by some legitimate law-giving authority and are subject to change. They attempt to apply the universal principle of the natural law to the concrete requirements of the traffic situation. As the circumstances change, the law-giver alters the regulations, always keeping in mind the natural law whose precepts the law-giver wishes to actualize. In the case of the ceremonial and judicial precepts, the law-giver is God whose enactment validates them.

REASONS FOR THE OLD LAW

Question 102 deals with "the causes of the ceremonial precepts" by which Thomas means the reasons behind the ceremonial precepts. Referring to Psalm 18:9, "The commandment of the Lord is lightsome, enlightening the eyes," and to Deut. 4:6, "This is your wisdom and understanding in the sight of nations," Thomas has no difficulty concluding that there are reasons behind the ceremonial precepts and that these reasons have to do with the end the law-giver is aiming to achieve. Thomas then embarks on a long and elaborate survey of the reasons for the precepts of the ceremonial law very much in the tradition of the Jewish *Ta'amei ha-Mitzvot* literature which devotes itself to explanations of the commandments of the Torah, especially those which do not appear "rational," at least at first sight. Maimonides was one of the most industrious practitioners of this enterprise and Thomas quotes Maimonides frequently as he goes about making the ceremonial precepts rational. As we cannot survey the whole project here, two examples will have to suffice. Referring to Exodus 23:19, "Thou shalt not boil a kid in its mother's milk," Thomas writes (102,6, Reply 4):

Admittedly, the kid that is killed is not affected by the way it is cooked, but it seems to savor of cruelty in man himself to use the mother's milk, given for the nourishment of her offspring, in the same dish. Or the reason could be that the Gentiles, in their idolatrous feasts, used to cook the kids' flesh in this way, either for sacrifice or for eating.

Thomas' explanation from idolatry corresponds to Maimonides' explanation in the *Guide, III,* 48.[2] With respect to the prohibition against wearing garments woven of linen and flax (Lev. 19:19), Thomas again (102,6, Reply 6) refers to "Gentiles, [who] in the worship of their gods, used garments of the sort, made of different materials. . . ." He adds: "The figurative reason is that the prohibition of garments woven of wool and linen means the prohibition of uniting the simplicity of innocence, denoted by wool, with the duplicity of malice, denoted by linen."

Thomas also distinguishes between the literal and figurative cause of the ceremonial precepts (102,2). He writes:

As we have seen, the reason for whatever is done in view of an end must be looked for in that end. Now the end of the ceremonial precepts was twofold; they were ordained for the worship of God at that time, and for prefiguring Christ, just as the words of the prophets had regard to the present, yet were also figurative of what was to come, as Jerome says. In the same way, then, the reasons for the ceremonial precepts of the Old Law may be taken in two ways. First, in relation to the divine worship to be observed at the time. In this aspect, they are literal, whether they concern the avoidance of idolatry, or the commemoration of particular divine benefits, or point to the divine excellence, or else indicate the frame of mind required of the worshipers of God. Secondly, their reasons may be assigned according to their purpose in prefiguring Christ. In this aspect, their reasons are figurative and mystical, whether they concern Christ and the Church—the allegorical sense, or the way of life of the Christian people—the moral sense, or the state of future glory to which we are brought through Christ—the anagogical sense.

In addition to the reasons for the ceremonial precepts that correspond to the kinds of reasons Jews gave, Thomas is also guided by the hermeneutics of prefigurement. Everything significant in the Old Testament must be read in two senses. "Now the end of the ceremonial precepts was twofold," he writes above; "they were ordained for the worship of God at that time, and for prefiguring Christ." Whatever meaning the narratives and precepts (laws) of the Old Testament may have had at the time they were given, they also had the probably more important function of prefiguring or foreshadowing the coming of Christ. "An animal that chews the cud and has a divided hoof," writes Thomas (102,6, Reply 1), "is clear in what it signifies; for the divided hoof signifies the distinction of the two Testaments, or of the Father and Son, or of the two natures in Christ, or of good and evil; and chewing the cud signifies meditation on the Scriptures and the right understanding of them." Speaking of the ritual of the red heifer (Num. 19:2) Thomas writes (102,5, Reply 5): "The figurative reason of this sacrifice is that the red cow signifies Christ in the lowly condition he took on himself, this being denoted by the sex of the animal; and its color signified the blood of Christ's passion." The prefigurative reading Thomas gives the Old Law will play a decisive role in his view on the duration of the Old Law.

DURATION OF THE OLD LAW

Having devoted a great deal of attention to the various aspects of the Old Law, Thomas in Question 103 addresses himself to the duration of the ceremonial precepts. That this question does not apply to the moral precepts of the Old Law follows from Thomas' conviction that the moral precepts of the Old Law correspond to the natural law which, as the moral law of reason, remains in effect as long as reason does. But this is not true of the ceremonial law, observance of which characterizes Judaism but not Christianity. The division of the Old Law into the moral precepts on the one hand and the ceremonial and judicial precepts on the other now proves its value. A portion of the Old Law, the moral, remains in full effect even after the coming of Christ while the ceremonial and judicial precepts are decisively altered, though not in the same way. "The judicial precepts," writes Thomas (104,3, Reply),

> were not binding forever, but were made void by the coming of Christ, though not in the same way as the ceremonial precepts. These became not only *dead,* but also *deadly* to those who should keep them after Christ had come, and particularly after the promulgation of the Gospel. The judicial precepts, on the other hand, are dead since they have no binding force, but not deadly. For should any ruler order their observance in his territory, he would not be committing a sin, unless they were observed, or ordered to be observed, as binding through enactment in the Old Law. To keep them on that ground would be mortally sinful.

The focus of the problem is therefore the ceremonial rather than the judicial precepts. While observance of both "as binding through enactment in the Old Law" would be mortally sinful, in the case of the judicial precepts there is a way of observing them which is not mortally sinful: if they are observed not "as binding through enactment in the Old Law" but as binding by enactment of a ruler who might enact all or some of these precepts as being useful and only coincidentally corresponding to precepts enacted in the Old Law. But this is not possible for the ceremonial law. To observe either the ceremonial or judicial precepts on the ground that to do so is in accordance with God's will is mortally sinful. The difference is that the judicial precepts may be observed as long as this is not done because God commanded them while this option does not exist with the ceremonial precepts observance of which is mortally sinful for any reason.

Thomas makes clear why the ceremonies of the Old Law ceased at the coming of Christ. He writes (103,3, Reply):

> All the ceremonial precepts of the Old Law were ordained to the worship of God, as we have said. Now the outward worship ought to be adjusted to the inward, which consists in faith, hope and charity; and so varied according to the variations of the inward worship. Of the latter, three states may be distinguished. The first regards faith and hope both of heavenly goods and the means of attaining them, in each case as to be had in the future; this was the state of faith and hope in the Old Law. The second is the state in which faith and hope are for heavenly goods as in the future, but of the means to them as in the present or past; this is in the state of the New Law. The third state is that in which both are possessed as present, and nothing is the object of faith as absent, nor of hope as to be had in the future; and this is the state of the blessed.

Commenting on this passage, David Bourke and Arthur Littledale write:

> The main point here appears to be that one of the two objects of faith and hope, namely the means of obtaining final salvation, is located at a particular point in history. To the men, therefore, who need to avail themselves of these means they are either future (for the men of the Old Testament), present (for those living in the time of Christ) or past (for those living in the time of the Church). The basic attitudes of faith and hope, therefore, vary according to whether the means of salvation are past, present or future in relation to the individual concerned. The man of the Old Testament must believe in and hope in the means of salvation as something which lies in the future, and the expression of his faith and hope in external forms of worship must manifest this. Such forms of worship must be "forward-pointing," oriented toward Christ as the goal of the covenant in Eichrodt's sense of the term (cf. his *Theology of the Old Testament I,* 6th ed., E.T., London, 1961, pp. 25–7). But for those for whom the Incarnation, Death and Resurrection of Christ as the essential means of salvation already lie in the past such es-

sentially forward-pointing expressions of worship are inappropriate. This is exactly the point which St. Paul makes so forcibly in the *Epistle to the Galatians*. To continue to perform the essentially forward-pointing works of the Law after Christ has come is tantamount to looking for some fulfillment of the Law other than Christ himself.[3]

It is here that the transformation from faithful obedience of the *mizvoth* to mortal sin occurs. Thomas writes (103,4, Reply):

> All ceremonies are professions of faith, in which the interior worship of God consists. Now a man may profess his inner faith by acts, just as by words; and in either way, if he professes something false, he sins mortally. The faith we have of Christ and that which the ancient fathers had is the same; but since they preceded Christ, and we come after him, this same faith is signified by us and them in different words. They said, *Behold a virgin shall conceive and bear a son* (Isaiah 7:14), using the future tense; we express the same by the past tense, saying that she *conceived and bore*. Likewise the ceremonies of the Old Law signified Christ as to be born and to suffer, whereas ours signify him as having been born and having suffered. Therefore, as a man would sin mortally who, in professing his faith, were to say that Christ was to be born, which the ancient fathers said devoutly and truthfully, so one would sin mortally who observed the ceremonies which those of old kept with devotion and fidelity.

To continue obeying the *mizvoth,* the commandments of the Old Law, after the coming of Christ is to deny that Christ has come and that is why it is mortal sin.

There is one final piece of the Thomistic mosaic about the Mosaic law that must be put in place before we can complete our exposition of Thomas' views on the Old Law. Were Jews justified by the Old Law prior to the coming of Christ? If the answer to this is positive, then the transformation brought about by the coming of Christ is decisive indeed. Prior to Christ, obedience to the law justified; after Christ it is mortal sin. But that is apparently too great a change, even for Thomas. The fact is that even before Christ, the Law did not justify. Thomas writes (103,2, Reply):

> As stated above, the Old Law distinguished two kinds of uncleanness: one spiritual, the uncleanness of sin; the other bodily, making a man unfit for divine worship. Thus a leper was held unclean, or anyone touching something dead; and this kind of uncleanness was no more than a kind of irregularity. From this uncleanness, therefore, the ceremonies of the Old Law had power to cleanse, since the Law itself prescribed them as the means to

remove the uncleannesses established by the Law. Hence St. Paul says [Hebr. 9:13] that *the blood of goats and of oxen, and the ashes of a heifer being sprinkled, sanctify such as are defiled, to the cleansing of the flesh.* And as the uncleanness in question was more of the flesh than of the spirit, the ceremonies themselves are called by St. Paul [Hebr. 9:10] *justices of the flesh, laid on them until the time of correction.*

From uncleanness of the spirit, however, they had no power to expiate; the reason being that there could never be expiation from sin except through Christ, who taketh away the sins of the world [John 1:29]. And since the mystery of Christ's incarnation and passion had not been enacted, those ceremonies of the Old Law could not have contained the power issuing therefrom, as do the sacraments of the New Law. Thus they could not cleanse from sin; as St. Paul says (Hebr. 10:4), *It is impossible that with the blood of oxen and goats sin should be taken away.* That is why he calls them [Gal. 4:9] *weak and needy elements;* weak, because unable to cleanse from sin, and the weakness is due to their being needy, that is not containing grace. The minds of the faithful, however, at the time of the Law, could be united by faith with Christ incarnate and suffering, and in this way be justified by Christ.

After the coming of Christ, presumably, "the minds of the faithful" could not longer be "united by faith with Christ" in the prefigurative sense. Because Christ had come, the choice was between explicit faith in Christ or implicit rejection of him by continuing adherence to the Old Law. The latter is therefore mortal sin. Before Christ, of course, adherence to the Old Law was not mortal sin but neither did it justify man before God. If man, before Christ, was justified it was only because the ceremonies of the Old Law prefigured Christ, and it is this union with Christ through the Old Law which pointed to him that justified man. In short, even before Christ it was Christ who justified man and not the Old Law. In turning into mortal sin after Christ, the Old Law did not turn from being a vehicle for justification into mortal sin but from being a vehicle that pointed to Christ—who justified—to a vehicle that denies Christ and is therefore the occasion of mortal sin.

EVALUATION

What can a Jew say about the position that is now, at least in its essentials, before us? It is clear that Thomas draws on the New Testament for his view of the Old Law. He writes (107,2,objection 3):

Anyone who acts contrary to a law does not fulfil the law. But Christ did many things contrary to the Law. For he touched a leper, and this was against the Law. Again, he seems to have violated the sabbath frequently, and so the Jews said of him (John 9:16), *This man is not from God, because he does not keep the sabbath.* Therefore Christ did not fulfil the Law.

But he soon qualifies this by writing (107,3, Reply 4):

Touching a leper was prohibited in the law because by it a man incurred a disabling defilement, as he also did by touching a dead man, as was said above. But the Lord, who was the cleanser of the leper, could not incur defilement. By acting as he did on the sabbath day he did not annul the sabbath in its true reality, as the Master himself showed in the gospel; for he worked miracles by divine power, which is always at work in the world, he performed works of human healing, while the Pharisees themselves provided for the healing of animals on the sabbath day, and he also excused his disciples for collecting ears of grain on the sabbath on the ground of necessity. But we may say that he annulled the sabbath in the superstitious meaning given to it by the Pharisees, who believed that one should abstain even from beneficial works on the sabbath; this was contrary to the intention of the Law.

This would seem to imply that Jesus violated superstitious misinterpretations of the Mosaic law rather than the true Mosaic law. The ambiguity in the Gospels with respect to Jesus' attitude to the law is thus reflected by Thomas.

Another question is whether Thomas' reading of Paul on the Mosaic law is substantially accurate. It seems clear that Thomas tried very hard to weave a consistent position out of the many, frequently at least apparently contradictory, things Paul says about the law. It seems to me that the increase in clarity we find in Thomas over Paul is due largely to the division of the Old Law by Thomas into the moral or natural law on the one hand and the ceremonial and judicial on the other. This division enables us to define exactly what remains binding after Christ and what has lost its force. And it is further true that Paul does speak of a law that the Gentiles "do by nature" (Rom. 2:14), a reference to some form of the natural law. But it is not at all clear to me that this rather passing reference to the natural law is meant by Paul to carry the weight that Thomas makes it carry in his theory of the Old Law. For Thomas, it is the natural law that enables us to slice the Old Law into a part that remains obligatory and a part that does not. This problem is particularly acute when we recall that the phrase that "it shall be a statute forever unto their generations" (Ex. 27:21 and elsewhere) occurs in the Old Testament in connection with such clearly ceremonial (in Thomas' sense) commandments as the pure olive oil that is to keep the lamp burning forever. We are thus left with two problems. First, even if it is legitimate to divide the commandments of the Old Law into those of the natural law which remain fully in force after Christ and the others which do not, how can we explain that the Old Testament attaches the phrase "it shall be a statute forever unto their generations" to precisely those commandments which according to the natural law criterion did not have permanent significance?

Second, we must ask how legitimate the natural law criterion as applied to the commandments of the Old Testament is. It is clearly not a criterion that is rooted in the Old Testament itself. The Old Testament knows only God's commandments and Israel's duty to carry them out. Whether those commandments seem rational or not does not seem to interest the Old Testament. While it is true that even in rabbinic literature an attempt was made to distinguish those commandments which man's reason can understand from those which it cannot, the rabbis were probably quite aware of the limitation on the usefulness of this distinction as they never made anything very significant depend on it. The rabbis, like the prophets, had no sympathy for those who were careful not to offend God but far less careful not to inflict injustice on man. But even the prophetic critique of sacrifices without justice was not meant to eliminate the sacrifices but rather to insist that they were not a substitute for justice. In short, the central role that Thomas assigns to natural law in his reading of the Mosaic Law seems more an imposition of medieval categories on the Pentateuch to which they remain extraneous.

The natural law doctrine, however, does not undermine the ceremonial law, it only fails to support the ceremonial law as permanently valid. The ceremonial law is undermined by its nature as a prefigurement of Christ, as we have seen. Here, two problems arise for the Jewish reader. The first is the very concept of prefigurement. That modern historical scholarship is partial to reading a text in the context of the language and culture of its place and time is not irrelevant to this situation. From a purely naturalistic standpoint, a document written in one epoch cannot be taken as referring to events hundreds of years in the future. At the same time, a believing Jew must understand that the naturalistic standpoint has its limitations when applied to sacred texts which, when divinely inspired, can prophesy (or foreshadow and prefigure) future events. Nevertheless, such non-naturalistic methods of interpretation ought to be used sparingly. When the Christian interpreter finds in the myriad details of the Jewish ceremonial law references to the birth, passion and resurrection of Jesus, the Jewish reader cannot help feeling uncomfortable. And most of all, when Thomas makes the prefigurement hermeneutics the foundation of his teaching of the annulment of the ceremonial law, the feeling of discomfort turns into one of positive distress.

For even if there is, from the point of view of Christian faith, a large element of prefigurement of Christ in the Old Testament, does it have to follow that someone who refrains from eating pork or who fasts on the Day of Atonement is committing a mortal sin? Must his action be interpreted as saying that "Christ was to be born" (103,4, Reply) rather than that he had been born, thereby denying Christ? Could adherence to the Mosaic Law not be interpreted much more benevolently, as love of God and his commandments, as fidelity to a holy way of life out of which—for Christian faith—the Redeemer was born? If the commandments before Christ predicted him, could they not after Christ celebrate the prediction that came true and point to the final fulfillment that both Jews and Christians await? In short, the argument that the Mosaic commandments predict Christ and that to adhere to them after Christ is a mortal sin because one is denying that he has come by so doing is a rather thin reed on which to hang the case for the ceremonial commandments turning into mortal sin after Christ. It is almost as if Thomas starts with that conviction and then looks around for some justification of it which he achieves by the ingenious argument of the prediction that turns into denial.

JEWS AND GENTILES

What drives Thomas in this direction? What forces him to the conclusion that obedience to the Mosaic Law—especially its ceremonial portion—is incompatible with belief in Christ? Ultimately it is a verse (Gal. 5:2): "If you are circumcised, Christ shall profit you nothing." This is the verse Thomas quotes in reply to the question, "Since the Passion of Christ is it possible to observe the ceremonies of the Law without mortal sin?" (103,4, Reply). Circumcision brings with it the whole of the Law, as the next verse (Gal. 5:3) makes clear: "For I testify again to every man that is circumcised that he is a debtor to do the whole law." If one is circumcised and therefore obligated to fulfill the commandments, one cannot benefit from Christ. If all this really means what it seems to mean, then it becomes necessary to conclude that adherence to the Mosaic Law is a mortal sin. But does it mean what it seems to mean?

The Mosaic Law can be handled in various ways. One way is to divide the Law into two portions, one of which remains in effect after Christ and the other that is superseded by the coming of Christ. This is the way Thomas approaches the subject. The difficulty with this approach, as we have seen, is that it then becomes necessary to separate the Law into various categories and that is not easy in view of the absence of such categories in the Pentateuch. But there is another division of which Thomas cannot be said to be unaware: the division between Jews and Gentiles. It is clear to Thomas that the Old Law, before Christ, was applicable only to Jews. Article 4 of Question 98 deals with the question "whether the Old Law should have been given to the Jewish People alone" and Article 5 asks "whether all men were obliged to keep the Old Law." Comparing the Jews before Christ to clergy, he writes (98,5, Reply): "Thus for instance certain observances are obligatory for clergy inasmuch as these are committed to the Sacred ministry, which are not obligatory for laymen." He adds, speaking of the Jews: "And it is in the same way that certain special obligations were imposed on that people, which were not imposed upon other people." So it is clear that Thomas has no difficulty with the concept that, before Christ, Jews were obliged to live up to a special set of demands not required of others.

It seems never to have occurred to him that all or some of these special demands required of Jews before Christ might remain obligatory after Christ. He seems to think that either the ceremonial Law, after Christ, is obligatory for all or it is mortal sin for all, Jew or Gentile. That the difference between Jew and Gentile might in some sense remain real after Christ never occurs to Thomas. To be more specific, he does not entertain the possibility that Jewish Christians ought to maintain a Jewish identity in the Church by continuing to live under the Mosaic Law, while sharing with Gentile Christians their faith in Christ. It is, after all, a fact that in Galatians and elsewhere where Paul polemicizes against the Law, he does so to *Gentiles* who have been persuaded that their Christian faith requires circumcision and the Law. Paul opposes this and, according to Acts 15, obtains the agreement of the Jerusalem Church that Gentile Christians need to obey only the Noachide laws. But the debate reported in Acts 15 could hardly have taken place if it was thought that Jewish Christians were no longer obligated to carry out all of the commandments of the Torah, including the ceremonial precepts. If because of the coming of Christ the ceremonial precepts were annulled for Jews, who could argue that they remained in effect for Gentiles? It is therefore clear from Acts 15 that all agreed on the continuing requirement to obey all the commandments for Jews after Christ. The debate centered on Gentiles who came to faith in Jesus. With respect to them, the decision was reached that the Noachide laws sufficed. But this, it seems to me, did not loosen the obligation of Jewish Christians to carry out the commandments of the Torah.

What prevented Thomas and Christians before and after him from seeing the law as remaining in effect for Jewish Christians but not for Gentile Christians? Probably texts such as Gal. 3:28: "There is neither Jew nor Greek, there is neither slave nor free, there is neither male nor female: for you are all one in Christ Jesus." This would seem to rule out any kind of Jewish/Gentile division in the Church. Yet, Paul could also rule that women were not to speak in the synagogue (1 Cor. 14:35) without this destroying the oneness of Christians in Christ. This ultimate oneness seems not to preclude penultimate differences in assigned tasks. Why, then, could Jewish Christians not be a kind of priesthood in the Church, subject to the demands of the Torah and in this respect differ from Gentile Christians who would be subject only to the Noachide law?

Another reason that this solution seems not to have commended itself to too many Christians is the conviction that the Old Law did not have the power to work justification (100,12, Reply). If it did not, then of what use is it after Christ? In the mind of Thomas, either the law justifies or it need not be obeyed. But that isn't necessarily so either. One can believe that only God can justify in the sense of forgiving sin and restoring the person to a state of innocence. But this does not have to mean that the law and its demands are no longer in effect. The law does not either justify or condemn but it states the norm. It is God's prerogative to forgive when the norm has been violated.

The teaching that obedience to the Mosaic ceremonial law after Christ is mortal sin not only strains Christianity's contemporary relationship with Judaism but needlessly weakens Christianity's bond with the Old Testament. It is clearly impossible for the Church to teach that this law is obligatory for all, Jewish and Gentile Christians. But it is less obvious why the Church could not either permit or require Jewish Christians to observe its requirements. Needless to say, the adherence to the Mosaic ceremonial law by non-Christian Jews would then also be evaluated more positively.

NOTES

1. *Paul, the Law, and the Jewish People* (Philadelphia: Fortress Press, 1983), p. 3.

2. Moses Maimonides, *The Guide of the Perplexed,* tr. Shlomo Pines (University of Chicago Press, 1963), pp. 598–601.

3. St. Thomas Aquinas, *Summa Theologiae,* Blackfriars Edition (New York: McGraw-Hill, 1969), v. 29, p. 242, footnote a.

IV. SCRIPTURE AS LITERATURE

Appreciating the Beauty
of the Bible

Clemens Thoma

We consider something beautiful if it appeals to us in such a degree that we feel captivated. Beauty thus exercises authority and influence. A person's life may be changed due to the charm flowing from a beautiful object and streaming toward him/her. A physically beautiful human being may similarly affect us by gaining influence and authority over us, altering our thinking and our actions. At all times, beauty holds innumerable dimensions and levels, but its atmosphere must be sensed rather than intellectually grasped.

When certain beings or objects have been accepted by many generations whose way of life was influenced and changed by them, then their beauty is confirmed independent of any rational analysis.

Such an experiential esthetics will serve as background to the following consideration of the Jewish and Christian Bible. We will ask if, why, and in what way Holy Scripture gains authority over us by its beauty.

1. SOME POINTS CONCERNING THE OUTLOOK
IN SCIENTIFIC RESEARCH

The Jewish thinker Franz Rosenzweig (1886–1929) wrote an essay on "The Mystery in the Style of the Biblical Tales"[1] one year before his death. In this essay he contradicts the view that there could never be a reconciliation between religious content and esthetic form. The Bible, he maintains, contains esthetic value of considerable force. If it was to be measured by categories of literary beauty, however, new points of guidance must be found. "The Bible is not the most beautiful book in the world, nor the most profound, truthful, prudent, exciting one, and no matter what further superlatives there may be;

none of them, in any case, will impress someone unless he/she be not already inclined toward them. Yet, the Bible is the most important book. This can be proved; and even the most fanatical antagonist must admit it at least in regard to the past, but by his aversion he proves it even for the present. There is no question here of personal taste, mental disposition or ideology; it is, rather, an issue of world history up to our time'' (178f). According to Rosenzweig, biblical tales can be fully considered categories of religious beauty only when listeners or readers are moved by them to active obedience, "into close view of Sinai,'' if these tales "turn into a point of departure for discourse'' (170f).

The Bible proved its dialogical influence on mankind's life and history, Rosenzweig claims, by its promise of salvation, its contradictions, its demands, and by exposing man's arbitrary behavior. The Bible thereby brought about new insights and developments, not so much by its epic tales but by the lyric poetry of the Book of Psalms, by prophetic rhetoric and legal casuistry. "Whenever the Psalms are recited, the Law being obeyed, the prophecies trusted, they shed at once the appearance of silent monologue and gain their voice, calling their Eternal Partner to a dialogue: man to listen, God to answer'' (180).

The biblical tales do not, according to Rosenzweig, assure continuous regeneration, as do the Psalms when they are activated and actuated in communal prayer. Yet, even between those tales and alienated listeners a mysterious "network of dialogue'' expands, and the tales "in the garment of their epic past preserve their full anecdotal power as tales of today. By questions and answers, dictions and contradictions, they endow those who are awakened to deeds, hope and love with that which is still lacking in them; and yet, giving humbly, they [the tales] do not dogmatically frustrate their hearers in action, in hope and love, but cause them to feel carried on spiritual wings'' (181).

When the Bible can ever and again be actuated and people of our time find their way to it and to its demands, thereby attaining to what they are meant to be as human beings, then certain literary categories of the Bible are at their pinnacle, then they are beautiful, says Rosenzweig. With this view, he has anticipated a great deal of modern communications theory. A holy text that does not appeal and does not effect change is without beauty and authority. It is probably not worth one's while unless one considers the Bible a mere object of scientific theories. Yet, if past generations were moved by the message behind the text which changed their life, that should be an impulse for religiously motivated people of our time to inquire into it.

In a letter to the Jewish scholar of biblical studies, Benno Jacob, Rosenzweig explains why so many parts of the Bible have influenced mankind up to the present day: "The Bible and our hearts express the same thing. For this reason (and for this reason only) the Bible is 'revelation.' ''[2] The Bible is the original mirror of a person's inmost soul; it is capable of disclosing and replying to the deepest yearnings and shortcomings of man's heart. The clarity and illuminating power of this mirror is its beauty and its authoritative force.

After the Second World War, the issue of biblical esthetics was raised again, in particular with regard to religious and linguistic-philosophical concerns. The peculiar nature of religious language was emphasized.

New Testament parables were at the center of discussion because a particularly high degree of literary and religiously evocative beauty was ascribed to them. Modern theological considerations became part of this review. Aristotelian logic will not lead anyone to intimacy and companionship with the God of the Bible. Rather, the most profound truths about God are held together and communicated to the world by a network of intimate relations (analogies, implications, allusions), between Creator and creation. The point is to make these consonances transparent to such a degree that people of our day may be motivated by them. Exegesis is adequate as long as it is capable of revealing the inspiring power of the sacred texts. It is effective when paying heed to the metaphorical character of all religious statements and its impact on religious groups and individuals.[3]

Dan O. Via and other scholars consider the New Testament parables autonomous, relational, esthetic objects, i.e., genuine works of art whose interpretation must set in at just that point. As window and mirror, the fully developed "work of art parable" mediates an application to the everyday world and confronts the reader with his own basic condition. In this way, he is led to inquire into the statements and demands of the parable. The latter should not be measured only by its revelational content but, first of all, by its secular and esthetic value.[4]

This and other attempts to improve understanding of religious texts with the help of esthetic categories is an imposing achievement. Yet, such an esthetic view overarching time and genre has not yet sufficiently taken root because the rules of literary esthetics may not be applied to religious writings without certain reservations.

Some brief examples from Jewish and Christian Scripture will demonstrate how the beauty of revelation may radiate and inspire, and yet at times may not prevail.

2. WHEN BEAUTY FAILS THE RELIGIOUS PERSON

The First Book of Maccabees, to Catholic understanding a biblical book, begins with a powerful description of Alexander the Great's invasion of the

Orient. Alexander had marched from West to East and conquered the mighty realm of Persia. In victorious campaigns he had plundered many nations and had advanced to the end of the world, until all the conquered nations threw themselves at his feet. Then, he turned into a haughty and supercilious person and set up a despotic rule. Soon afterward however he fell ill and, feeling at death's door, divided his colossal empire among the army commanders who after his death crowned themselves kings.

These Diadoches brought great misery upon the entire world of those days. One of the most godless and wicked descendants of that Greek dynasty turned out to be Antiochus IV Epiphanes (175–164 BCE). The Jews suffered so much from his oppression that traitors to the Law turned up who persuaded many Jews to abandon God and the faith of their fathers (1 Macc 1:1–15).

That chapter, though written by a Jewish patriot, is typical for Greek historians in the classic sense. Not one phrase is superfluous, every word goes to the point, the dramatic effect is convincing. We must remember here that the Bible contains few "classic" chapters of history. Apart from the religiously disputed Books of Maccabees, there are two biblical portions only that are not confined to the history of Israel but relate to the history of the nations. They are the so-called Genealogy (Gen 10) and Daniel 11 (the veiled telling of history from the time of the Persian Empire to Antiochus IV Epiphanes).

In the previously cited articles by Franz Rosenzweig, on the other hand, he indicates that the Pentateuch stories are not history writing in the classic sense; and just for that reason they are religiously impressive and effective. Anecdotes, legends, fairy tale motives, historical reminiscences, symbolic acts, catastrophes, deeds of liberation, etc. form a literary palette of surprise and mystery. They are far more appealing than classic historical writing because they address the topic and the reader in a religiously evocative manner.

History as related at the beginning of the First Book of Maccabees may gladden and inspire a modern historian but it cannot fan religious enthusiasm, much less could it move a person of our time to confront the God of Israel and His Will. It can do no more than make us ponder human arrogance, which does not require revelational scripture. The underlying historical assumption that with Antiochus IV's reign the nadir of the world's history was reached has become quite obsolete in our time.

3. RELIGIOUS BEAUTY IN SECULAR GARB

The Hebrew Book of Esther (*Megillat Esther*) is the only biblical book that presents its religious message in secular language. The word "God" never occurs. Even when dealing with religious customs, such as the time of fasts, festivals, giving of alms (Est 3:6; 9:19–28), no direct religious reasonings or allusions are expressed but only discreetly implied. On the grounds of its non-religious diction and some episodes apparently exposing a Jewish inclination toward revenge (Est 7:8–10; 9:1–16), the Book of Esther remained disputed for a long time. In TB*Meg* 7a, all the rabbinic arguments for or against the Book of Esther are summarized, whether or not it should be considered inspired by the Holy Spirit.

R. Yose ben Durmasqit introduced the following reasoning for its acceptance. It is said in Est 9:10, ''But they laid no hand on the plunder.'' In the Book of Esther, so we can interpret R. Yose, a small step toward a better world order was taken. Haman's people wanted to attack all the Jews and their property (3:13). After the Jews had been saved from Haman's clutches, the situation was reversed, and they could have paid back with equal coin (9:1). Yet, the Jews did not commit the serious sin of seizing their murdered enemies' possession.

Acceptance of the Book of Esther is best substantiated by Est 9:27, ''The Jews stood up for it and accepted it.'' That is interpreted to mean: '' 'They stood up for it'—above (in Heaven); 'and accepted it'—below on earth (the people of God)!'' Rav Yosef, in support of the arguments in favor added Est 9:28, ''And those days of Purim will never be forgotten by the Jews.'' That argument was, indeed, the final answer because it expresses Rabbinic pragmatism: The Book of Esther was accepted as Holy Scripture because it had become very dear to the Jewish people. If the people of God had come to love it, it is also dear to God.

Yet, why did the Jewish people take so much pleasure in the Book of Esther that they kept, and keep even to this day, the obligations implied therein? The question of authorship as well as the historical hour of its writing and the transparency of the narrative may lead us to an answer. An unknown Jew, well acquainted with the religious and political miseries in the region of Jerusalem, was in a position to understand the deadly danger which the tyranny of the Hellenistic Seleucids posed to the Jews in Judea and Jerusalem. Under Seleucos IV (187–175 BCE), the Temple treasure was variously plundered and the Jewish people exposed to many annoyances. In the first years under Antiochus IV, the religious and cultural assaults upon the Jews worsened (cf Dan 2–6; 11). The said Oriental Jew wanted to warn his Jewish countrymen in the disguised style of a tale from Persia: Be on guard! You must expect cruel persecutions by Antiochus IV. The author particularly intended to address those Jews who had succeeded in becoming influential dignitaries within the Hellenistic political power system and had concealed their Jewish identity from their pagan masters. The beautiful Esther who, on order of Mordechai at first did not reveal her Jewish descent (Est 2:10.20), serves the author as the prototype for successful Jews who were trying to save their own skin, regardless of persecutions and sufferings of their own people (4:13f). It was these influential Jews in their selfish ambition whom the author wanted to exhort to give up their selfishness and stand by their hard pressed people. Their powerful positions should enable them to help and to save. Yet must they avoid rash actions but rather proceed with caution and circumspection, exactly as Queen Esther did in the tale (Est 5–7).

Prudent and effective solidarity with the oppressed people of God is the central topic of the Book of Esther; it is not treated in a generalized way, though, but firmly placed within the context of other biblical messages. Particularly significant and heightening the drama is the fact that the theme is made to hearken back to the biblical Amalek tradion. The anti-Jewish Haman is represented as "Agagite," i.e., Amalekite (Est 3:1.4.10). When he hears that Mordechai, who will not bow to him, is a Jew, he makes up his mind to destroy him together with all the Jewish people (Est 3:6).

The Amalek tradition is the most terrifying of all the Old Testament. When Israel first came to doubt the nearness of God (Ex 17:7), Amalek appears as the first enemy of the people. There ensues a war which through the prayer of Moses is won by Israel. Then follows a harsh prophecy of enmity: "The Lord will have war with Amalek from generation to generation" (Ex 17:16). Relentless enmity between Israel and Amalek was impressed upon Israel as an obligation (Dt 25:17–19). Israel must never forget what the arch-fiend Amalek had done to them in the days of the Exodus. In 1 Sam 15, King Saul the Benjamite is reproached for not having waged total war against Agag, the king of Amalek, and instead, with lame excuses, had saved much of the booty. The Benjamite Mordechai, however—according to the tale in Esther—realized the dangerous nature of the Amalekites of his days and did his utmost to destroy them.

Amalek of the Bible is the code word for cruel, antagonistic forces against God and Israel. The Book of Esther won in actuality because shortly after its writing a new Haman, or Amalek, emerged: Antiochus IV Epiphanes. It developed that the Amalek-Haman threat turned up over and over again and that the Jews could not expect to live in peace. In the history of a later time, Hitler had to be identified with Amalek-Haman.

More than being but a testimony to Jewish identity and history, the Book of Esther also has a particular literary transparency and subtlety. When reading or hearing the tales of the Esther Book, any Jew with some links to Jewish tradition becomes immediately aware of the fact that its secular language is a mere veil drawn around a religious message. The message applies to each individual Jew as well as to the whole Jewish people, and the relationship between individuals and the people. Jews are also aware that non-Jews do not understand the hidden allusions to Jewish history and an actual situation. This esoteric-sapiential element also strengthened the ties between Jews and this strange Holy Scroll.

The fate of the Book of Esther (*habent libella sua fata*) demonstrated the important part the people of God was to play in the development of the Bible. Esther was accepted as Holy Scripture by the Jewish people because this book is an indication of the typical destiny of this people, its enduring peril, because the book is full of cryptic literary references, and because it is in its very concept a vigorous appeal to be on guard against the enemies of God and man. For these reasons, religious truth and beauty gleam within all the parts of the Book of Esther. Its truthfulness forever draws the attention of mankind to an ever latent threat to Jewish identity and existence among the Gentiles. The Book of Esther also paves the way for a religious message, to turn mankind away from error and egoistic indifference.

What we have described here is a kind of beauty pointing far beyond mere historical description; and it is realized whenever the Purim festival is celebrated and wherever human beings prudently defend themselves against surrender of their religious and national identity.

4. RELIGIOUS BEAUTY IN UNPOPULAR STATEMENTS

General canonical approval to the New Testament Epistle of James was not given until about 400 CE. In the the time of the Early Church already there ensued difficulties over its acceptance as Holy Scripture. Even after canonization, these troubles were not over. In the 16th century, Martin Luther called the Epistle of James, the Book of Esther and 2 Maccabees "too Jewish" and that it would be better not to include them in Holy Scripture. He called the Epistle of James "mere straw", and he maintained that some Jew who "wanted to put something over," must have written the Letter.[5]

The Epistle of James contains many unpopular statements which at various times aroused suspicion among Christians. It says in Jas 3:1, "Let not many of you become teachers, my brethren, for you know that we who teach shall be judged with greater strictness." These are words to check ideological enthusiasts of the Early Church who believed unconditional confession of the dogma of the Crucified and Resurrected Christ is the only strength of Christianity and who endeavored to develop the Church as a kind of para-Jewish master and disciple organization. Even the central Jewish confession of faith, the Sh'ma Israel, however, was relativized by James: "You believe that God is one; you do well. Even the demons believe and shudder" (2:19).

Actually, James did not attach overly much importance to right believing but rather to right doing, namely, love of neighbor (cf. 2:24). In some other respects also James cut through the thicket laid by ideologists and novelty fanatics. He emphasized again and again, and with deliberate partiality, the bond between the Jewish tradition and faith by doing. In his writing, James introduces Abraham, the whore Rahab, and the prophet Elia according to Jewish interpretation (2:21–26; 5:17f): and it is not Jesus who is named as model of patient suffering but Job (5:11). It is obvious that James opposes the severing of the Church from her Jewish roots.

In our post-Holocaust time, we are able to realize the disastrous consequences of separating Christianity from Judaism and its active piety. We also begin to see how hostile to religion ideologies can be. This makes the Letter of James a piece of Scripture no longer to be overlooked, and even early Christians or Martin Luther would no longer turn up their nose at it. Its unpopular tendency against separation and religious ideology is of high religious-esthetic value and thereby religiously effective, quite apart from the question whether the book also has literary beauty. After our recent experience of transgressions against the Jewish people and the evil that ideological, fanatical thinking may bring over humankind, the Letter of James holds undiminished religiously evocative force in our time.

5. FURTHER ASPECTS OF RELIGIOUS BEAUTY

The New Testament and Rabbinic writings most significantly show how the religious and esthetic power of Old Testament revelation was modified, so as to adapt it to a different era and its problems. Scholars of Christian theology as well as of general theology and literature tend to consider the New Testament parables an outstanding example of the enduring power of biblical revelation in a new garment. In order to demonstrate that this also applies to Rabbinic parables, we shall briefly discuss here that particular genre.

The Rabbinic parable consists of comparison, symbols, metaphors, and allegories, and in its metaphoric structure it presents an uncomplicated, profane, fictional narrative. Such a narrative, containing a plot, does not stand on its own merits but serves the exegesis of the Oral and Written Law (*Torah she be' al-Pe* and *Torah she bi-Ketav*), as interpreted by the Rabbis. The story was usually invented or recomposed by a narrator well acquainted with the Torah, with the intention of disclosing and explaining a meaning or precept implied in a particular passage of the Torah or to make that passage more intelligible.

The parable is not addressed to an individual and does not refer to any particular event. It is meant to serve the common religious, liturgical or halakhic teaching of Jewish communities. The narrator takes into consideration that these communities no longer live in biblical times but rather need impulses pertaining to their present day needs.

As a metaphoric structure, on one side profane (*mashal*), on the other relating to revelation (*nimshal*), the Rabbinic parable extends into the limited and ever-changing world of human experience, as also into the unlimited and eternal world of revelation. This can be illustrated schematically by a circle (a closed figure as likeness to a profane narrative) and a parabola (open toward infinity as likeness to revelation). Circle and parabola are located on two different isotopic planes, that of human experience and that of the world of revelation. These two planes do not touch, yet they give light to and reflect one another. The parable of the King's Wine is an impressive expression of such an interdependence.[6]

Rabbi Berekhia told in the name of Rabbi Levi:

Like unto a king
who owned a vineyard,
and handed it over to a tenant.
When the vineyard produced good wine,
the king used to say:
How good is the wine
of *my vineyard*!

Likewise the Holy One, blessed be He,
said in the beginning
to Moses:
"Come now therefore
and I will send thee unto Pharao,
that you mayest bring
my people, the children of Israel
out of Egypt" (Ex 3:10).

But when it produced bad wine,

the king used to say:
How bad is *my tenant's* wine!

But after Israel did
that unspeakable deed of theirs,
what did He say?
"Go thee down, for *thy people*
have dealt corruptly" (Ex 32:7).

Whereupon the tenant replied:
My lord king!
When the vineyard produces
good wine,
you say:
How good is the wine
of *my vineyard*!?

Whereupon Moses replied:
Master of Universes!
When the children of Israel sin,

they are called *mine*!

But when it produces bad wine,
you say:
How bad is the wine
of *my tenant*!?

But when they are free of sin,
they are called

Thine!?

Yet good or bad, the wine is *yours*!	Yet sinful or sinless, they are *Thine*! "They are Thy people and Thine inheritance" (Dt 9:29). "Destroy not Thy people and Thine inheritance" (Dt 9:26). "Lord, why does Thy wrath burn against Thy people" (Ex 32:11)?

Content

King → God. Vineyard → Israel. Tenant → Moses. To own a vineyard → to make Israel in Egypt God's own. To give the vineyard to tenants → to give Israel in the care of Moses. To produce good wine → to be obedient to God at the Exodus. To produce bad wine → to sin against God by worshiping the Golden Calf.

This parable gives a very clear picture of the tension between course and structure of the narrative and its encoded message.

mashal Surface text = level of profane experience (actors and allomotifs)	*nimshal* Deepness text = level of Revelation (actants and motifemes)	Structure of the plot
King owns a vineyard King hands over the vineyard to the tenant.	God chooses Israel God entrusts Israel to Moses	Preliminaries
Vineyard produces good wine. How good is the wine of *my vineyard*!? Vineyard produces bad wine. How bad is the wine of *my tenant*!?	Israel is obedient on Exodus. God inclines toward Israel. Israel sins (Golden Calf). God leaves Moses with Israel alone.	Plot with misleading perspectives
Tenant's reply: Good or bad, both are the king's wine.	Moses reply: in obedience *and* in sin, Israel remains God's possession.	Clue: God is not like man.

The true meaning of the parable is not disclosed before the very last sentence of the *mashal* and *nimshal*. At first glance, both texts seem to suggest that God judges and acts just like human beings, by laying the blame for disagreeable things on somebody else. In the course of the profane narrative and its transposition to the works of God with Moses and Israel, statements disguising the true situation and misleading perspectives are used. It is made to appear as if God acts like a human proprietor who wants to use only the good parts of His possessions while charging failures to His subordinates. He must be made aware of His wrong attitude by the accused. Like a human owner, He does not question His proprietorship (the vineyard) but only the bad produce (the wine). Applied to God's relation to Israel, this means that He loved only an obedient Israel at the Exodus. When Israel worshiped the Golden Calf, He had dismissed them from His love and had forsaken them. Yet, He was cunning enough to acknowledge Israel as His possession.

On the level of the profane narrative already, the tenant begins to unmask the dubious situation; in fact, his reply to the landowner is unseemly. This is a prelude, however, to Moses' statement on God's true manner of acting toward Israel. God is not in analogy with a human vineyard owner. God loves and accepts Israel unconditionally—even in their most serious sin. Using a surprising twist, the parable teller creates in the hearer or reader an *Aha* experience. Not even sin can drive away the love of God. The parable now stands unveiled as indirectly antithetical; it has an antithetic structure and an ironical ductus. Only after having been deceived by paradox, the reader/hearer has the whole truth revealed to him: God is not like human beings.

The parable of the King's Wine was held to be beautiful by Jews of all times because it contains a strong, impressible, almost dramatic message of consolation. Christians and Muslims over and over again accused the Jews of stubbornness and wickedness. The parable, however, announces that God is superior to the Israelites' sinfulness. He remains faithful even, and particularly so, when Israel sins. He does not forsake them in their sinfulness but continues to keep them as His own people.

6. CONCLUSION

This brief survey of religious esthetics with all its authority and force leads to the conclusion that sacred literature is not dependent on literary beauty. Such writings contain an internal agent capable of bringing about change in human beings. To this effect, they must be transparent (from the divine to the human level, and vice versa) and truly verifiable in the course of historical events. They must have communicative value beyond their linguistic garment. Sacred writings must reflect the divine so as to appeal to and move the human *sensus religiosus*. Holy literature should, moreover, confirm historical religious experience so that human beings become better and more prudent, or at least will be given an impulse in that direction. The religious-esthetic charm of the Old Testament, the New Testament, and the Rabbinic writings is alive even in our day.

NOTES

1. Franz Rosenzweig, "Das Formgeheimnis der biblischen Erzaehlungen", in *Kleinere Schriften* (Berlin, 1937), pp. 167–181.

2. *Idem, Briefe und Tagebuecher,* Rachel Rosenzweig *et al.,* eds. (Den Haag, 1979), II, 708f.

3. Cf. Dan O. Via, *The Parables* (Philadelphia, 1967); Paul Ricoeur, Eberhard Juengel. "Metapher, zur Hermeneutic religioeser Sprache," in *Evangelische Theologie,* special issue (Munich, 1974); Wolfgang Harnisch, ed., "Die neutestamentliche Gleichnisforschung im Horizont von Hermeneutik und Literaturwissenschaft," in *Wege der Forschung* 575 (Darmstadt, 1982); Anselm Haverkamp, "Theorie der Metapher," in *Wege der Forschung* 389 (Darmstadt, 1983); Manfred Kaempfert, "Probleme der religioesen Sprache," in *Wege der Forschung* 442 (Darmstadt, 1983).

4. Cf. John D. Crossan, *Finding Is the First Act* (Philadelphia, 1979). Also: Clemens Thoma, Simon Lauer, eds., *Die Gleichnisse der Rabbinen,* Erster Teil: Pesikta deRav Kahana (PesK), Uebersetzung, Parallelen, Kommentar, Texte (Bern: Peter Lang, 1986), Series Judaica et Christiana, vol. 10. One hundred and thirty-three Rabbinic parables are analyzed and compared with other narrative units. The Institute for Judaeo-Christian Research in Lucerne, Switzerland plans to publish within the next few years, all the Rabbinic parables (about eight hundred), with commentaries.

5. Martin Luther, *Table Talk,* III, 254; *Prolegomena to the New Testament* (EA 63, 115).

6. B. Mandelbaum, *Pesikta deRav Kahana* (New York: Jewish Theological Seminary, 1962) I, 227f.

Humanistic Understanding of Scripture*

Simon Lauer

Erasmus of Rotterdam started writing on Psalms when an opportunity to do so presented itself in 1515. Later on he may have thought of an all-embracing work; this, however, never materialized. Erasmus occasionally turned to it at various moments of his life. One purpose of his whole endeavor becomes clear from the following quotation: ''I fiercely oppose those people who do not want Holy Writ translated into a vernacular to be read by non-specialists [*idiotae*]; whether Christ's teachings were so involved as to be understood by very few theologians only, or the Christian religion could be protected only if it be ignored.''[1]

Elijah Levita, in a sense a humanist, had a Judaeo-German translation of the Psalms printed in Venice in 1545 for women and uneducated persons, trying in this way to impart a meaning to the spare hours of his fellow Jews.

Things became more complicated in 18th-century England. There, the question arose whether Psalms should be translated for liturgical usage or rather be replaced. In the former case, too many church-goers could not be expected to understand what they were singing, owing to the obscurity of those oriental poems.[2]

In Germany, Johann David Michaelis not only translated Robert Lowth' epoch-making ''De sacra poesia Hebraeorum'' but published also a translation of the Psalms in 1771 under the telling title, ''Teutsche Uebersetzung des alten Testaments, mit Anmerkungen fuer Ungelehrte.'' Besides this concern for the common reader, Michaelis joined in the effort to draw attention to the beauty of the Bible as proof of its divine origin. Moreover, he wanted to provide pastors with some help in interpretation and in the stylistic improvement of their sermons.

Michaelis had a Jewish ally in his striving for undogmatic exegesis,

Moses Mendelssohn. He not only shared Michaelis' scholarly concern; to him "the unbiased humanistic approach to the Psalms [also] meant the breaking down of the barriers of prejudice."[3] A decade later, a certain shift of emphasis seems to have taken place, viz. from the struggle for undogmatic exegesis to the striving for an individual, inward *mea res agitur*. In Mendelssohn's own words: "To me it seems that many [sic] Psalms are of the sort that they must be sung with true edification by the most enlightened people."[4]

1. FACTORS UNDERLYING HUMANISM

On February 26, 1517, Erasmus wrote to Capito: "There is still one scruple besetting me: Lest paganism tried to raise its head under the clothing of ancient literature reborn . . . lest Judaism thought of rising to life again, when Hebrew letters become reborn. There is nothing more adverse and nothing more hostile to Christian doctrine than this latter disease."[5] For the former fear there were obvious reasons. Moreover, while the non-allegorized *sensus humilior* ought not to disappear, it must not be isolated either; otherwise it may lead to "judaizing," i.e. understanding Scripture literally, and this would amount to killing the spirit. For a proper understanding of the *mysterium* Christi, the leap into faith is required.[6] Thus, Erasmus' humanism works out to be basically Christian, Christ being the normative image of true Man.

In a sense, Mendelssohn was closer than Erasmus to the more pagan side of Renaissance humanism, since he ascribed the same dignity to truth, goodness, and beauty as forming the essence of humanism, while beauty definitely meant less to Erasmus than truth and goodness. Of course, Mendelssohn also had a normative "image of true Man" but this was not in any way the image of an historical person with a definite proper name.[7]

2. PHILOLOGY WITHIN THE LIMITS OF THEOLOGY

While Erasmus certainly thought of philology as a discipline on which theology depends—much more so than on philosophy—he would not have considered philology to be a *conditio sufficiens* for theology.[8] In any case he would have rejected the opinion, as uttered in the 18th century, that hermeneutics rested on philology rather than on the Holy Spirit; the professor of biblical exegesis taking over authority from the Pope or the Church's tradition.

When reading Erasmus, one should bear in mind that literary devices were not an end in themselves for him; rather were they to be considered a means for persuasion, basically indifferent as to their value from a strictly theological point of view: "God does not take offense at solecisms, but he is not pleased with them either. He hates presumptuous eloquence, this I grant you; but much more so supercilious and arrogant stammer."[9]

Still, we feel that a theological issue might possibly be involved in Erasmus' esthetics: Maybe, he declares, you will find things in Plato's and Seneca's books and Socrates' life which are not abhorrent to the Christ's teachings and his life; but this harmony of all things congruent with one another all around, you will find in Christ alone.[10] "This harmony [viz. of Scripture with Christ] is not disturbed by Christ's variety; on the contrary: Just as an appropriate composition of diverse voices makes for a sweeter accordance, so Christ's variety renders the accordance fuller."[11] This would seem to point to the dogma of Trinity.

The well-known humanistic call "to the sources," moreover, has to be viewed in close connection with the concepts of *humanitas* (ethics and love of peace), *libertas* (freedom from ceremonial law), and *simplicitas* (the liberating force of divine simplicity as realized in Holy Writ).

Allegory is allotted a place of pride in Erasmus' exegesis. Its functions are summarized by Tracy.[12] One of these is providing the letter of Holy Writ with a spiritual meaning in case it be not evident by itself. There seems to be a sort of proportion: Spiritual meaning is to literal what *libertas* is to the ceremonies. This would seem to be one of the most efficient causes of Erasmus' "theological antisemitism," much deplored in modern times.[13] There is, of course, no excuse for this. Some aspects of Erasmus' violence against Jews and Judaism, however, must not be lost sight of.

It has not been a very long time yet since controversies, even among educated people, have been carried out according to polite rules. Commonplace patterns of polemics as inherited from antiquity still seem to come to the fore now and then. Finally, rather early in its history Christianity definitely left the framework of Judaism in order to solicit the support of educated heathens. Hence there exists a rather close connection of Christianity with humanism, despite theological quandaries arising from this connection. Erasmus quite obviously wished to be a Christian; in no case would he have liked being a barbarian.[14]

At the end of his interpretation of Psalm 39, Erasmus grants freedom for allegory, provided the latter is handled with skill and learning, even if its results work out to be mistaken. A sincere scholar, however, would not just utter what may be said as occasion offers itself, but what comes nearest to truth in accordance with the general sense of the whole literary unit.[15]

3. AIMS AND METHOD OF LITERARY CRITICISM

Jewish scholars such as the Kimhis have developed as early as the 12th century the method of paraphrasing difficult biblical texts. This method allows the verse to explain itself, once it has been restructured.[16] Although Erasmus despaired of applying this method to the Psalms generally, after having tried it on Psalm 3, he somehow came back to it in his treatment of Psalm 118, where he paraphrased some twenty different verses from other Psalms in order to teach, please, and move the reader.[17]

When the "obscurity" of biblical texts became a problem for the classicist mind of the 18th century, paraphrase was widely used as a means either for supplying what was felt as lacking in the original, or for omitting the seemingly superfluous, and in general for discreet hints at an esthetic criticism which believing Englishmen at the time would refrain from voicing explicitly.[18]

Was it only "teutonic openness"[19] which gave Mendelssohn the courage to contest the poetic quality of some Psalms in much the same terms as English and French critics applied? It seems that this openness was rather a result of the striving for an undogmatic reading of Scripture which in turn became possible owing to a fresh evaluation of God-given reason.

Mendelssohn, while certainly sensitive to grammatical and stylistic problems, was far from being enthusiastic about textual criticism as it was put forward in his days.

On one short page of his Preface to the Reader which precedes his translation of the Psalms, Mendelssohn uses the word "critical" no less than four times. He assures the reader that he has never departed from his predecessors "without critical reason," that he has translated "without critical prejudice" and wants to be read and judged "without critical prejudice." Finally, he promises to accept correction "without critical obstinacy." It appears that in the three last instances "critical" has a pejorative sound. The first occurrence, on the other hand, points to the work of literary taste and criticism—an *analogon rationis* in terms of the philosophy to which Mendelssohn adhered.[20]

Erasmus was criticized for "preferring science to faith."[21] Maybe one could accuse Mendelssohn of preferring philosophical esthetics to the pious routine of ordinary people.[22] Although Mendelssohn did his work on the Psalms when the beginning "age of genius" was ready to dispense with learned commentaries altogether, he still made ample use of the more rationalistic among the great classical Jewish commentators, such as Abraham ibn Ezra and David Kimhi. As for Erasmus, his preferred authority was Origen, but especially so for the latter's non-theological contribution to biblical scholarship, since Erasmus was careful not to fall into ingenuousness, especially when it donned the garb of Aristotle.[23]

4. CHANGING APPROACHES TO SCRIPTURE

Erasmus begins his *Enarratio* of Psalm 1 with a statement of the difference between divine and human wisdom, divine and human language. Psalms are not like Homeric hymns; one is not allowed to approach them in a state of impurity. Although one cannot grasp Scripture without an effort, a proper understanding is granted to those only who piously search for it (*piis vestigatoribus*). For this, however, the purity of heart as granted by baptism is indispensable.[24]

Erasmus in some way anticipated later ideas. His *Encheiridion militis christiani* was reprinted in 1699 in Halle. Early Pietism was sensitive to the undogmatic Christianity of practical ethics, loving-kindness, and simplicity of heart, as advocated in this work. A.H. Francke, the initiator of pietist exegesis, demanded "experience" (*Erleben*) of the Bible as a prerequisite for rebirth which, in turn, was the only guarantee for a proper understanding. This vindication of subjectivism was to lead in due course to a mainly esthetic view of the Bible.[25]

Before commenting on Mendelssohn's Preface to the Reader, J.B. Loewe urges the reader to sing the Psalms that have been selected by our Sages for liturgical purposes, in a pleasant and orderly manner; else no sensation (*Empfindung*) would be possible which, in turn, leads to joy.[26] This criticism of thoughtless recitation of Psalms reminds one of Erasmus' criticism of the mechanical prayers which he witnessed when still a monk at Steyn.[27]

The preceding considerations lead us to the problem of the relationship between divine inspiration and human exegesis, which was so forcefully advanced by Hamann, Mendelssohn's great antagonist[28] (cf. Kirchschläger, this volume, for the situation in our time).

If Erasmus had already achieved a far-going liberty vis-à-vis the text of the Bible, as appears from his all-important concern with a correct text based on ancient testimonies rather than on *Masora,* to which Mendelssohn still held, the dogma of verbal inspiration was considerably softened around the year 1700. According to Francke, the writers of Scripture were not tools without a will but illuminated by the Holy Spirit, not *extra se rapti*. Instead of looking for a scholarly norm of interpretation, therefore, one had to read Scripture with the same affect which one felt the writer must have had. This affect was entirely dependent on the reader's emotion, not on the standard of his education.[29]

Hamann went even farther in qualifying the methods of philological interpretation: the context or scope of a given scriptural passage was not all-important. Obscure passages were understandable for those persons only to whom they turned out to be addressed—"non solum totaliter aut collective sed distributive . . . Ecclesiae singulas partes et animas fidelium irrigandas."[30]

As we have seen, Mendelssohn's reading of Scripture, besides being a matter of pure thinking, depended as far as biblical poetry was concerned on literary taste. Sensation (*Empfindung*) achieved the rank of a divine creation.[31] This was to lead up to what I would call an osmosis of poetry sacred and profane. While Scripture gained the esthetic importance of poetry *tout court,* it lost its meaning in terms of revelation, whereas profane poetry underwent a process of sacralization.

So it would appear that, as time went on, readers of Holy Scripture felt more and more concerned as individuals, whereas in Erasmus' time a proper understanding of Scripture still largely depended on objective criteria—a view which was to live on.

5. CONCLUSION

In conclusion, we could define humanistic exegesis as an exposition of the moral (theological) meaning of a text accounting for its overall sense, its context and setting, and its literary quality.

A humanistic reading of Scripture would mean (1) to establish a philologically sound text; (2) to interpret a text in its setting and to look for its original scope; (3) to apply the results of such investigations to the spiritual and temporal well-being of the individual ("edification") and society as a whole (ethics, love of peace) alike.

A reading of Scripture may not be described as humanistic if it uses isolated biblical passages as proof texts irrespective of their context and original scope, considers obscurity of the text a positive value since obscure passages must be understood as prophecies addressed to individual readers only, and strives to experience (*erleben*) Scripture rather than to interpret it.

Both readings are founded on the basic assumptions of the divine character (whose exact meaning may vary considerably) of Scripture, and of human freedom of investigation, the latter being limited by the requirements of scholarly method for the humanist, and by a particularly strong sense of piety for the non-humanist.

NOTES

*Alexandro Altmann—mentori, praeceptori—discipulus.
1. "Paraclesis," in *Desiderius Erasmus Roterodamus, Selected works,* H. & A. Holborn, eds., 1933–1964, p. 142.
2. R.P. Lessenich, "Dichtungsgeschmack und althebraeische Bibelpoesie im 18. Jahrhundert," in *Anglistische Studien* IV, 10–12 (1967).
3. Alexander Altmann, *Moses Mendelssohn. A Biographical Study* (Univ. of Alabama Press, 1973) p. 244.
4. Letter to Sophie Becker, cf. Altmann, *loc. cit,* p. 719.
5. *Opus epistolarum Des. Erasmi Roterodami denuo recognitum et auctum,* Percey Stafford Allen *et al.,* eds. (Oxford, 1906–1958) II, 491.
6. G. Chantraine, S.J., "Erasme, lecteur des Psaumes," in *Colloquia Erasmiana Turonensia* (Paris) II, 696 (1972).
7. Alexander Altmann, "Das Menschenbild und die Bildung des Menschen nach Moses Mendelssohn," in *Mendelssohn Studien* (Berlin) I, esp. 26 (1972).
8. G. Chantraine, S.J., " 'Mystère' et 'Philosophie du Christ' selon Erasme," in *Bibliothèque de la Faculté de philosophie et lettres de Namur* XLIX, 243 (1971).
9. Erasmus, "In Novum Testamentum praefationes, Apologia," in *Ausgew. Schriften,* G.B. Winkler, ed. (Darmstadt, 1967) III, 114.
10. *Loc. cit,* "Ratio seu Methodus," III, 220.
11. *Loc. cit.,* p. 222
12. J.D. Tracy, "Erasmus. The Growth of a Mind," in *Travaux d'humanisme et renaissance,* CXXVI, 127–166 (Geneva, 1972).
13. J.-C. Margolin, "Erasmus, Declamatio de pueris statim ac liberaliter instituendis. Etude critique, traduction et commentaire," *Travaux d'humanisme et renaissance* LXX, 89–93 (Geneva, 1966). G. Kisch, "Erasmus' Stellung zu Juden und Judentum," in *Philosophie und Geschichte* LXXXIII/IV (Tuebingen, 1969).
14. R. Pfeiffer, "Humanitas Erasmiana," in *Studien der Bibliothek Warburg* XXII, 24 (London, 1931).
15. "Enarrationes in Psalmos," in *Desiderii Erasmi Roterodami opera omnia,* ed. 1703–1706, V, 468D/E.
16. F.E. Talmage, *David Kimhi. The Man and the Commentaries* (London/Cambridge, 1975), p. 61.
17. G.B. Winkler, "Das Psalmenargument des Erasmus im Streit um den freien Willen," in O. Fatio/P. Fraenkel, eds., "Histoire de l'exégèse au XVIe siècle, *Etudes de philologie et d'histoire* XXXIV (Geneva, 1978), 106.
18. Lessenich, *loc. cit.,* pp. 126, 128.
19. *Loc. cit.,* p. 225.
20. Altmann, *Menschenbild,* p. 24
21. A. Godin, "Fonction d'Origène dans la pratique exégétique d'Erasme: les annotations sur l'Epître aux Romains," in Fatio-Fraenkel, *op. cit.,* p. 38.
22. Especially as far as the perusal of the Psalter is concerned, cf. J.B. Loewe,

Commentary on Mendelssohn's translation of the Psalms (Hebrew) 1791, ²1799, 3rd Preface, p. 7.

23. Chantraine, *Psaumes, loc. cit.*, p. 697.

24. *Loc. cit.*, p. 702,

25. D. Gutzen, "Poesie der Bibel. Beobachtungen zu ihrer Entdeckung und ihrer Interpretation im 18. Jahrhundert," Diss. phil. (Bonn 1968, 1972), pp. 42f.

26. Loewe, *loc. cit.*

27. Quoted by C. Béné "L'exégèse des Psaumes chez Erasme," in Fatio/Fraenkel, *op. cit,* p. 120.

28. J. Dyck, *Athen und Jerusalem. Die Tradition der argumentativen Verknuepfungen von Bibel und Poesie im 17. und 18. Jahrhundert* (Munich, 1977), p. 118. Gutzen, *loc. cit.*, p. 89.

29. Dyck, *loc. cit.*, p. 116.

30. S.-A. Jørgensen, "Hamanns hermeneutische Grundsaetze," in R. Toellner, ed., *Aufklaerung und Humanismus. Wolfenbuetteler Studien zur Aufklaerung* VI (Heidelberg 1980), p. 221. Hamann's quotation from: James Spedding *et al.*, eds., *The Works of Francis Bacon* (London, 1858, reprint Stuttgart-Bad Cannstatt, 1963), I, 836.

31. Gutzen, *loc. cit.*, pp. 109f.

Notes on the Contributors

DAVID BERGER is Professor of History at Brooklyn College and the Graduate School of the City University of New York. He is the author of *The Jewish-Christian Debate in the High Middle Ages*, which was awarded the Medieval Academy of America's John Nicholas Brown Prize for 1983, and of numerous articles on Jewish-Christian relations and the intellectual history of the Jews. He is co-author (with Michael Wyschogrod) of *Jews and 'Jewish Christianity'* and editor of *The Legacy of Jewish Migration: 1881 and Its Impact*, and *History and Hate: The Dimensions of Anti-Semitism*.

MAURICE GILBERT, S.J. is Director of the Pontifical Biblical Institute in Jerusalem and Visiting Professor at the Ecole Biblique e Archéologique Française in Jerusalem. Previously Rector of the Pontifical Biblical Institute in Rome. Editor of *Biblica*. Publications are *La critique des dieux dans le Livre de la Sagesse*; (with J.L'Hour and J. Scharbert) *Morale et Ancien Testament;* editor *La Sagesse de l'Ancien Testament;* articles in *Dictionnaire de la Bible, Documentation Catholique,* and others.

WALTER KIRCHSCHLÄGER is Professor for New Testament at the Catholic Theological Faculty, Luzern, Switzerland. Previously at the University of Vienna, Austria. He published *Commentary to the Constitution "Dei Verbum," Gedeutetes Wort, Die Paulusbriefe vorgestellt, Jesu exorzistisches Wirken aus der Sicht des Lukas, Schriftverstaendnis leicht gemacht, Die Evangelien vorgestellt.*

SIMON LAUER is Research Fellow of the Institute for Judaeo-Christian Research at the Catholic Theological Faculty, Luzern, Switzerland. Ph.D. in Classics and Semitics. Co-author (with Clemens Thoma) of *Die Gleichnisse der Rabbinen, 1st vol.: Pesiqta deRav Kahana,* editor of *Kritik und Gegen-kritik in Christentum und Judentum,* contributor to *Journal of Jewish Studies, Freiburger Rundbrief, Judaica, Theologische Realenzyklopaedie.*

JORGE M. MEJIA is Bishop of Apollonia and Vice President of the Pontifical Commission on Justice and Peace; previously Secretary of the Vatican Commission for Religious Relations with the Jews. Also served as Secretary to the Department for Ecumenical and Interreligious Relations of the Latin American Council of Bishops, and was Peritus during the Second Vatican Council. He was editor of *Criterio* and has published extensively.

NAHUM M. SARNA is currently Professor Emeritus, was Dora Golding Professor of Biblical Studies at Brandeis University. Departmental editor and contributor to the *Encyclopaedia Judaica,* articles in *Encyclopaedia Britannica, Encyclopaedia of the Middle Ages,* and *Encyclopaedia of Religions.* He is the author of *Exploring Exodus* and *Understanding Genesis.* He was an editor and translator for the Jewish Publication Society Bible Translation, and is general editor of its Bible Commentary. Fellow of the American Academy for Jewish Research, former fellow at the Institute for Advanced Studies at the Hebrew University, Jerusalem.

EDWARD A. SYNAN, Priest of the Roman Catholic Archdiocese of Newark, N.J. Prelate of Honor to His Holiness. Fellow of the Royal Society of Canada, Professor and past-President, Pontifical Institute of Mediaeval Studies, Toronto, Professor Emeritus of the University of Toronto. Author of *The Works of Richard of Campsall, The Popes and the Jews in the Middle Ages,* translator of *The Fountain of Philosophy, Fons philosophiae of Godfrey of Saint Victor.*

FRANK TALMAGE teaches medieval Jewish civilization and Hebrew in the Department of Near Eastern Studies, University of Toronto. He is the author of *David Kimhi: The Man and the Commentaries,* and of the forthcoming edition of the Proverbs commentaries of the Kimhi family. He has also written and edited studies on various medieval biblical commentaries and theological works.

CLEMENS THOMA is Professor for Biblical Sciences and Judaic Studies at the Catholic Theological Faculty of Luzern, Switzerland, Director of its Institute for Judaeo-Christian Research. Co-author (with Simon Lauer) of *Die Gleichnisse der Rabbinen, 1st vol.: Pesiqta deRav Kahana;* (with Michael

Wyschogrod) of *Das Reden vom einen Gott bei Juden und Christen; A Christian Theology of Judaism; Die theologischen Beziehungen zwischen Christentum und Judentum;* co-editor of *Freiburger Rundbrief, Theologische Realenzyklopaedie;* numerous articles in German and Swiss theological periodicals.

MICHAEL WYSCHOGROD is currently Professor and Chairman of the Department of Philosophy at Baruch College of the City University of New York; Director of the Institute for Jewish-Christian Relations of the American Jewish Congress. He has taught at a number of American and European universities and contributed to many scholarly journals. Among his books are *The Body of Faith: Judaism as Corporeal Election,* and *Kierkegaard and Heidegger: The Ontology of Existence.*

Index

Kara, A. 92
Kaspi, J. 84
Katz, J. 54f
Kaufmann, Y. 60
Kayserling, J. 100
Keller, W. 34
Keywords 56ff
Kimhi, D. 14f, 18, 156
Kimhi, J. 89, 100
Kirchschlaeger, W. 45
Kisch, G. 159
Kotler, A. 60
Kuenen, A. 24

L

Lagrange, J. 32, 64
Latourelle, R. 46
Lectio Divina 70
LeDeaut, R. 67
Leibowitz, N. 60
Lémonon, J. 77
LeMoyne, J. 77
Léon-Dufour, X. 72
Lessenich, R. 159
Levine, E. 67
Levita, E. 153
Lieberman, S. 96
Literal sense 16
Literary, aesthetics 143; criticism 156; genres 69
Literature 37f
Liturgical poetry 68
Loewe, J. 157, 159
Loewe, R. 17, 20
Lohse, E. 45
Loisy, A. 32
Lombard, P. 88
Loyola, I. 63f
Lubac, H. 35, 74
Lunshitz, R. 52
Lupo, T. 35
Lustiger, Card. 104f
Luther, M. 59, 152

M

McCarthy, D. 76
Mckenzie, J. 45
Maccabees 143
Magisterium 40, 75
Maimonides 16, 126ff
Mandelbaum, B. 152
Manns, F. 35

Margolin, J. 159
Meanings, multiplicity of 10, 25f, 44
Medieval Jewish, exegesis 17; study 81f
Mendelssohn, M. 154; and text criticism 156
Methods of exegesis 21ff
Michaelis, J. 153
Milgrom, J. 61
Mit brennender Sorge 71
Modernism 22, 32
Moral sensitivity 51, 54
Moral superiority 51
Mussner, F. 77

N

Nahmanides 14, 16, 49
Natural law 109, 127, 134f
Neo-fundamentalism 55
Neusner, J. 31
N.T. and O.T. 70f
Noachide laws 137
Noah 109
Nostra Aetate 66

O

O.T. and N.T. 70f

P

Parable 142, 148; of king's wine 149f
Paraphrase 156
Patriarchs, and bible criticism 54; immunity of 53
Paton, L. 59
Penkover, J. 19
People of the book 81
Permissiveness 52
Peshat 16
Petahiah b. Jacob 83, 96
Pfeiffer, R. 159
Philology and Theology 154
Pietism 157
Poetry, sacred and profane 158
Polemics 49ff
Political dimension of dialogue 4
Pontifical Biblical Institute, study rules of 64ff; publications of 72
Pope, M. 20
Potterie, I. 32
Precepts, Jewish 108f, 119, 127, 130f
Prefiguration 129, 135
Presuppositions, of exegesis 24ff
Proleptic nature, of text 17
Psalm reading 92

Psalms 142, 156
Punishment 56

Q
Quality of bible study 88

R
R. Eliezer ha-Gadol 85
R. Gershom 85
R. Tam 84f
R. Yose b. Durmasqit 145
Rabbinic, exegesis 10, 12; Judaism 81; tradition 31; transformations 12
Rahner, K. 46, 103ff
RashBaM 18
Rashi 18, 59, 86, 95, 99
Ratio Studiorum 64ff
Rawidowicz, S. 19
Relative perfection 126
Religious Language 143
Revelation 39f
Ricoeur, P. 152
Rosenthal, E. 98
Rosenthal, J. 50, 58
Rosenzweig, F. 141ff, 152
Rosh ha-Seder, J. 83
Roth, C. 63
Rudloff, L. 122
Ryle, H. 13, 20

S
Sabbath 113
Salvation 112, 118
Samuel b. Hofni 18
Sanders, E. 125
Sarna, N. 19, 31, 61, 99
Schneiders, J. 20
Scholarly interaction 4
Scholastic interpretation 116
Scholem, G. 10, 19, 97
Schuermann, M. 33
Scriptural scholarship, context of 69, 94f
Scripture, dialogical character of 44; exposition of 10; inspiration and 36ff, 42; literary beauty of 143, 151; as literature, 37; numinous quality of 92; role of 81; senses of 114; spiritual value of 89; study of 10, 21f, 84; Talmud and 81ff; tradition and 9, 22ff, 25, 40f; unity of 71
Sephardim 82
Sheshemites 50
Sin 118

Skinner, J. 14, 20
Smalley, B. 98, 107, 124
Smend, R. 45
Solidarity 146
Song of Songs 112
Spirit and Scripture 28, 42
Stereotypes 3
Strack, H. 35
Study program 64
Study questions 76
Stuhlmacher, P. 33
Supersession 102f
Sykes, D. 57, 60
Synagogue, status of 111
Synagogue/Church separation 106

T
Talion 71
Talmage, F. 97, 159
Talmud, study of 84
Tension, divine/human 40
Tetragrammaton 12
Thoma, C. 77, 152
Thomas Aquinas 114ff, 125ff
Tosato, A. 76
Tracy, J. 155, 159
Tradition 72f; and text 16, 21, 25, 70
Training program 64
Tree, sacred 12ff
Twersky, I. 99

U
Urbach, E. 98

V
Vaccari, A. 74
Vatican II and Scripture 41
Via, D. 143, 152
Vigouroux, F. 72

W
Weil, G. 67
Wellhausen, J. 24
Wieder, N. 96
Wilenski, M. 97
Winkler, G. 159
Wistinetzki, J. 59, 97
Witness people 111
Written text, and moral truth 15

Z
Zimmels, H. 96f

Stepping Stones to Further Jewish-Christian Relations: An Unabridged Collection of Christian Documents, compiled by Helga Croner (A Stimulus Book, 1977).

Helga Croner and Leon Klenicki, editors, *Issues in the Jewish-Christian Dialogue: Jewish Perspectives on Covenant, Mission and Witness* (A Stimulus Book, 1979).

Clemens Thoma, *A Christian Theology of Judaism* (A Stimulus Book, 1980).

Helga Croner, Leon Klenicki and Lawrence Boadt, C.S.P., editors, *Biblical Studies: Meeting Ground of Jews and Christians* (A Stimulus Book, 1980).

John T. Pawlikowski, O.S.M., *Christ in the Light of the Christian-Jewish Dialogue* (A Stimulus Book, 1982).

Martin Cohen and Helga Croner, editors, *Christian Mission-Jewish Mission* (A Stimulus Book, 1982).

Leon Klenicki and Gabe Huck, editors, *Spirituality and Prayer: Jewish and Christian Understandings* (A Stimulus Book, 1983).

Leon Klenicki and Geoffrey Wigoder, editors, *A Dictionary of the Jewish Christian Dialogue* (A Stimulus Book, 1984).

Edward Flannery, *The Anguish of the Jews* (A Stimulus Book, 1985).

More Stepping Stones to Jewish-Christian Relations, compiled by Helga Croner (A Stimulus Book, 1985).

STIMULUS BOOKS are developed by Stimulus Foundation, a not-for-profit organization, and are published by Paulist Press. The Foundation wishes to further the publication of scholarly books on Jewish and Christian topics that are of importance to Judaism and Christianity.

Stimulus Foundation was established by an erstwhile refugee from Nazi Germany who intends to contribute with these publications to the improvement of communication between Jews and Christians.

Books for publication in this Series will be selected by a committee of the Foundation, and offers of manuscripts and works in progress should be addressed to:

> Stimulus Foundation
> 785 West End Ave.
> New York, N.Y. 10025